DoubleSpace
Without the DoubleTalk

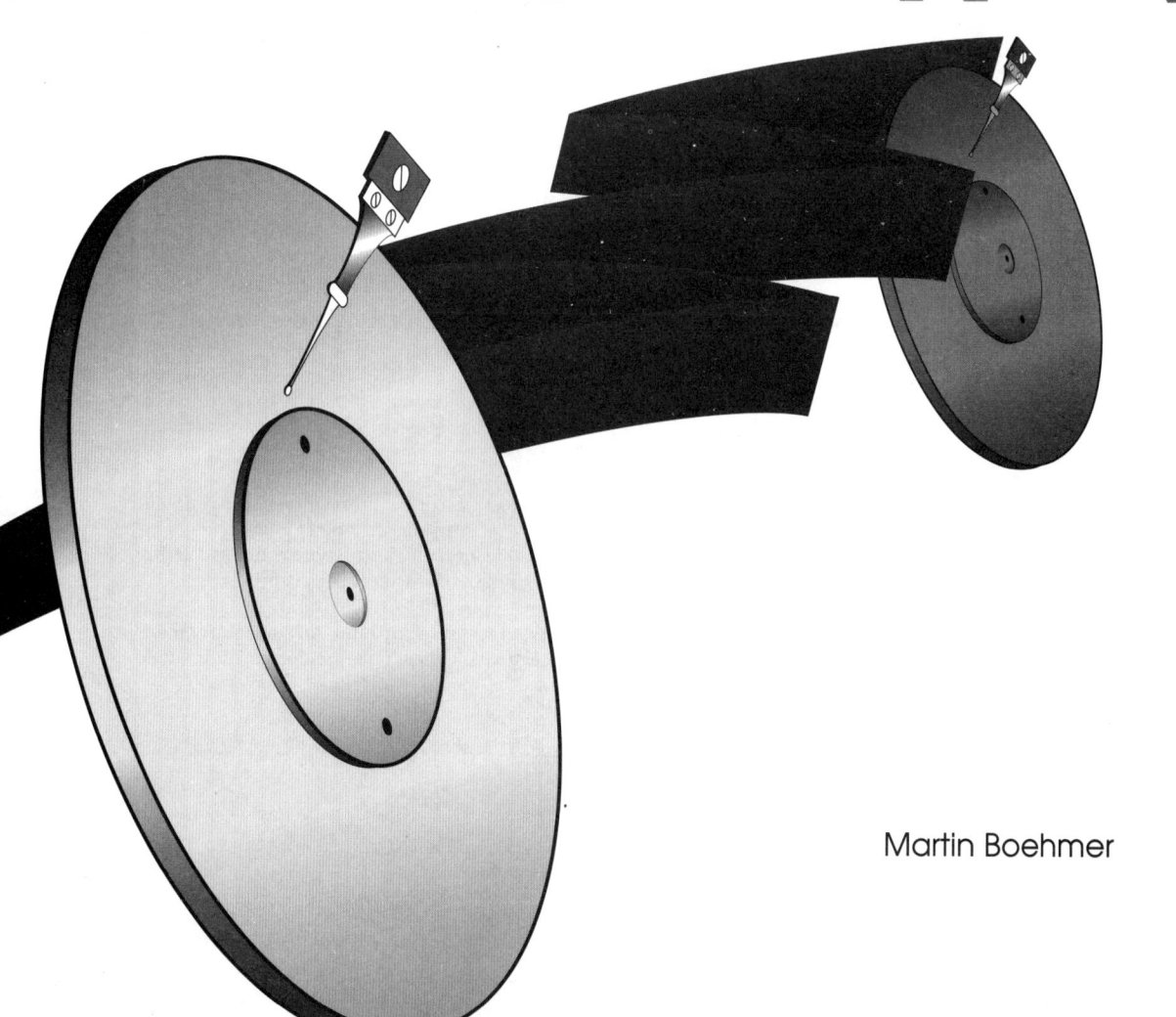

Martin Boehmer

Abacus
A Data Becker Book

Copyright © 1994   Abacus
                    5370 52nd Street SE
                    Grand Rapids, MI 49512

Copyright © 1993   Data Becker, GmbH
                    Merowingerstrasse 30
                    4000 Duesseldorf, Germany

Managing Editor: Scott Slaughter
Editor: Louise Benzer
Technical Editor: George Miller
Book Design: Scott Slaughter
Cover Art: John Plummer
Proofreader: Robbin Markley

This book is copyrighted. No part of this book may be reproduced, stored in a retrieval system, or transmitted in any form or by any means, electronic, mechanical, photocopying, recording or otherwise without the prior written permission of Abacus Software or Data Becker, GmbH.

Every effort has been made to ensure complete and accurate information concerning the material presented in this book. However, Abacus Software can neither guarantee nor be held legally responsible for any mistakes in printing or faulty instructions contained in this book. The authors always appreciate receiving notice of any errors or misprints.

This book contains trade names and trademarks of several companies. Any mention of these names or trademarks in this book are not intended to either convey endorsement or other associations with this book.

Printed in the U.S.A.

ISBN 1-55755-250-9

10 9 8 7 6 5 4 3 2 1

Quick Contents

Chapter 1
Introduction to Data Compression — 1

Chapter 2
Data Compression In Detail — 13

Chapter 3
Before Compressing Your Hard Drive — 27

Chapter 4
DoubleSpace — 81

Chapter 5
Stacker 3.1 — 133

Chapter 6
Inside DoubleSpace — 203

Chapter 7
Glossary — 225

DoubleSpace Without the DoubleTalk

Contents

Contents

1 Introduction to Data Compression — 1

What Is Data Compression? 3
    Data compression basics 4
    Data compression uses 4
Methods Of Data Compression 5
Data Compression Advantages and Disadvantages 6
Data Compression Programs 8
Selecting A Compression Program 9
Hardware and Software Requirements 10

2 Data Compression In Detail — 13

Logical and Physical Drives 15
Partitions 16
RAM Drives 17
Compressed Volume Files (CVFs) 17
Host Drives 18
Compression Factor 18
Compression Ratios 20
Compression Speed 21
Fragmentation 22
Cross-linked File Clusters 23

viii DoubleSpace Without the DoubleTalk

Contents

Memory Types	23
Memory Management	25
Protecting Your Data	25

3 Before Compressing Your Hard Drive   27

FDISK	29
FORMAT	34
Creating a boot diskette	35
CHKDSK	36
DEFRAG	37
BACKUP	39
MSBACKUP for DOS	39
Restoring data	50
MSBACKUP for Windows	54
Restoring data	63
BACKUP and RESTORE	65
MEM and MEMMAKER	70
MEMMAKER	72
Manual changes	75
ScanDisk (DOS 6.2 and above)	78

4 DoubleSpace   81

Installing DoubleSpace	83
Checking partitions	83
Deleting unnecessary files	85
Removing CHK files	87
Defragmenting	87
Starting the installation	88
Optimizing memory	95
Converting compressed drives to DoubleSpace format	95

DoubleSpace Without the DoubleTalk

Contents

Using Compressed Drives 97
    MS-DOS 98
    MS-Windows 100
Managing Compressed Drives 101
    DoubleSpace interface 102
    Changing the drive size 105
    Changing the compression ratio 108
    Formatting compressed drives 109
    Deleting compressed drives 110
    Defragmenting drives 111
    Compressing diskettes 112
Optimizing Your Hard Drive 116
    More space for the hard drive 116
    More free RAM 117
    Higher access speed 117
    DBLSPACE.INF 118
    DBLSPACE.INI 121
DOS 6.2 Additions 122
DoubleSpace and Other Applications 123
    Cache programs 124
    Windows swap file 124
    EXTDISK.SYS device driver 125
    Drive device driver 126
    Compressed files 126
    Windows NT Flexboot System 126
    Novell networks 127
    DOS DEFRAG 128
Common Error Messages 128
Removing DoubleSpace 131
Uncompressing Drives (DOS 6.2) 132

DoubleSpace Without the DoubleTalk

Contents

5 Stacker 3.1 — 133

Installing Stacker 135
    Checking partitions 135
    Deleting unnecessary files 137
    Removing CHK files 139
    Defragmenting 139
    Converting a DoubleSpace drive 150
Using Compressed Drives 152
    MS-DOS 153
    MS-Windows 155
Managing Compressed Drives 157
    Stacker for DOS 157
    Stacker for Windows 169
Optimizing the Hard Drive 175
    More space for the hard drive 175
    More free RAM 176
    Higher access speed 177
    Stacker Tuner 177
Stacker and Other Applications 179
    Cache programs 179
    Windows swap file 180
    Compressed files 181
    DOS DEFRAG 181
Common Error Messages 181
Removing Stacker 183
Uncompressing Drives 184
Stacker Command Lines 185

DoubleSpace Without the DoubleTalk

Contents

6 Inside DoubleSpace — 203

Command Lines 205
Extensions in DOS 6.2 214
The DoubleSpace API 217
    Calling methods 217
    INT 2Fh calls 217

7 Glossary — 225

Index — 235

CHAPTER 1

Introduction to Data Compression

Contents

What Is Data Compression? 3

Methods Of Data Compression 5

Data Compression Advantages and Disadvantages 6

Data Compression Programs 8

Selecting A Compression Program 9

Hardware and Software Requirements 10

Introduction to Data Compression

Chapter One

If you're confused about what data compression is and how it's used, then you'll find some answers in this chapter. We'll discuss what data compression actually means, the different methods of data compression, the dangers associated with data compression, what compression programs are available, and which program is right for you. You'll also find some information on the hardware and software that's needed in order to use data compression.

What Is Data Compression?

Data compression has actually existed for quite awhile in the computer world. Originally, data compression was an important part of data transmission. One of the main purposes of data transmission is to make transferring information more effective and affordable. This can be done by either increasing the speed of transmission or decreasing the amount of data that must be transmitted.

However, both of these methods have limitations. For example, if the data is transmitted over a commercial telephone network, you must remain within certain transmission rate limits. Line noise and other considerations may cause you to lose data.

On extremely noisy telephone lines, error correction protocols may not be efficient. The time spent re-transmitting imperfectly-received data cancels out any gains made by using a higher transmission rate. Also, the receiver must be able to process the high transmission rate. Many older modems are able to work at only lower baud rates. (Bauds are bits per second.)

Data density can be increased only within a limited range. One method involves sending the data telegram style. This means that all unnecessary letters and punctuation marks are omitted. However, when numerical sequences and specific data, such as addresses, program code, or graphics, must be transmitted, this method cannot be used.

Because of the problems with both of these methods, data compression was developed.

Introduction to Data Compression

Chapter One

Data compression basics

Data compression doesn't increase the data density by omitting unnecessary information, eliminating repetitions, or minimizing data errors. Instead, similarities in the data structure are used to consolidate portions of the data temporarily. This process isn't performed on the letters used in language; instead it's used with bits and bytes. Repetitions are found much more frequently on this level.

For example, to us the number 11 isn't a repetition or duplication. Otherwise, we wouldn't be able to distinguish 1 from 11 or from 111. In other words, each of these numbers is a separate entity.

Several zeros and ones on the bit-level can be combined into new complete character sequences. Different methods are used in compressing data in this way, so that any body of compressed data will only be decipherable with the compression program that was used to compress the data. Therefore, the act of compressing is also a type of encoding procedure.

During decompression (i.e., when the data is transformed back into its original state), the compression program replaces the complete sequences of compressed bits and bytes with the combinations of ones and zeroes which represent the original data.

The advantage of data compression and decompression over simply abbreviating and simplifying data is that when you create data (e.g., with a word processing, database, or graphics application), you don't have to worry about the amount of data. Therefore, incomprehensible abbreviations or line drawings aren't necessary because the data can be compressed in its full form.

Data compression uses

In addition to data transmission, data compression is also used for backing up data. So a backup won't take unnecessarily large amounts of magnetic tape or countless diskettes, the data is compressed during the backup process. During a subsequent restore operation (i.e., when the data is rewritten onto the hard drive from the backup copies), the same data is decompressed. Since the backup process stores the data in compressed form, it isn't possible to return the data to your hard drive using the DOS command COPY, for example.

Introduction to Data Compression

Chapter One

A newer use for data compression is in archiving large amounts of data or also permanently storing data. The most common example of this method is the program diskettes of most software manufacturers. For example, if an application takes 31 Megabytes of storage space on your hard disk, such as Corel Draw, it could take up 31 separate diskettes to hold the necessary information.

In this case, installing this application on your computer would be a tedious process. Therefore, the application's program files are compressed using an archiving program (which is simply a compression program) and stored on the program diskette(s) in complete form.

In the case of Corel Draw, this decreases the amount of diskettes by almost 20. During the installation, the data on these diskettes is then restored to its full size. The compression that is used makes it impossible to use a simple copy program to move the program data from the program diskettes onto your hard drive.

Today data compression is often used to store drawing and graphics archives as well as other types of data that must be stored for various reasons. This creates more room on the hard drive while still allowing quick access to the data via the decompression program.

Methods Of Data Compression

Today the different types of data compression are divided into two categories: Online and Offline.

In Offline compression, the data is first compressed, and then sent over a data net. Once the data reaches its destination, the packed data is decompressed in another separate step. This type of compression is normally used for compressing program diskettes. The manufacturer compresses the data and distributes it onto the diskettes. During installation the compressed files on these diskettes are moved to the hard drive.

The files are then decompressed from there because of its higher operating speed. Only poorly programmed installation programs will decompress their data directly from the floppy onto the hard drive. In these cases, the

Chapter One

Introduction to Data Compression

installation program is often simply a decompression utility. Archiving programs also use offline compression. First the data is stored normally, and then it's placed into the archive via compression.

Compression and decompression for backup operations, however, use online methods. Here the data are compressed onto the backup diskettes on the fly (i.e., while the data is being written). Otherwise,

> **Note**
> For more information about offline archiving refer to PKZip, LHARC, & Co by Abacus.

there wouldn't be sufficient disk space. Therefore, two separate tasks run simultaneously during online compression: Backup and compression.

An example of a special type of online compression is the compression of the contents of an entire hard drive. Every read and write operation to the hard drive is intercepted by a compression program. Everything that is written onto the hard drive is first compressed.

Therefore, anything that is read from the hard drive must also be decompressed before it's passed on to the application that accessed the drive. This type of online compression is used by programs, such as DoubleSpace, Stacker, and DoubleDensity. Therefore, we'll focus on this method of compression.

Data Compression Advantages and Disadvantages

The advantages of data compression are obvious. The most important advantage is that you can reduce the amount of storage space needed to store a given amount of data, while retaining the data's integrity. This process saves hard and floppy disk space.

There are also other advantages. For example, compressed files can be copied more quickly than their full-sized versions. Therefore, it's easier and less time-consuming to copy diskettes. Also, sending compressed files through electronic data transfer can reduce the transmission times, in comparison to the uncompressed files, up to fifty percent. This can also

Introduction to Data Compression

Chapter One

reduce the number of errors that can occur during the transmission, because less data is being transmitted. As a result, transmission costs are also reduced.

However, there are also some disadvantages to data compression. One disadvantage of online data compression is that more time is needed whenever a file is saved or loaded. To minimize these wait times as much as possible, you should use a fast PC and hard drive. However, it's also possible to use compressed hard drives on less powerful PC systems, at least under DOS. (For more information, refer to the "Hardware And Software Requirements" section in this chapter.)

Also, you should compress only less frequently used files, instead of system or program files that you use regularly. (We'll discuss this in more detail in the chapters on individual applications.)

Finally, you should use an operating system version that permits the use of hard drive partitions of more than 32 Meg, since even a compressed 20 Meg drive will result in 40 Meg of disk space (exceeding the 32 Meg limit). If you're using DOS 3.3, you must partition the hard drive into two separate partitions (more about this in the "Hardware And Software Requirements" section in this chapter), which means additional unnecessary work.

Data compression becomes more hazardous if other applications are also influencing read and write operations or are accessing the hard drive directly. Usually these applications are memory-resident virus checkers, as well as actual viruses, and all hard drive optimizers, such as PC Tool's COMPRESS or Norton's DEFRAG.

However, usually the manufacturers of compression programs either have made sure that these types of programs can't create problems (or that they simply won't work) or that they cooperate with the compression. However, you must be careful with compression programs from other unknown sources. If you're using one of these programs, if possible perform tests before entrusting it with valuable data.

Compressed hard drives are defragmented through the special tools of the compression programs, so you won't need to use a PC Tools or Norton Utilities defragmenter.

Introduction to Data Compression

Chapter One

Finally, there is also a possibility of losing data because of a power failure. However, compressed disks aren't lost completely if this occurs. Only the file that was open when the power was cut will be damaged or destroyed. This is also what happens to non-compressed disks in this situation.

Compressed drives are compatible with most software applications, user interfaces, such as Norton Commander, PC Tools, operating system supplements, such as Windows, and of course DOS. Special commands aren't needed. Compressed drives work the same way as non-compressed ones.

Data Compression Programs

There are almost as many data compression programs as other types of applications. The following is a brief overview of the types of programs that are available:

- DOS 6, the newest version of the operating system, includes its own online data compression program called DoubleSpace.

- User Interfaces, tools, and utility collections that are equipped with offline compression programs, such as the Norton Commander (DOS), Norton Utilities (DOS and Windows), as well as PC Tools (DOS and Windows).

- Archiving programs, such as LHArc, HardDrive, and Zip. There are also DOS utilities that are available free or for a small fee as shareware.

- Online compression programs that double hard drive capacity. These include Stacker (DOS and Windows) and DoubleDensity (DOS).

- Applications that are equipped with their own compression tools. For example, Corel Mosaic, the graphics file manager for Corel Draw, compresses its files in an archive.

Introduction to Data Compression

Chapter One

- Backup programs, regardless of whether DOS Backup or backup tools by other manufacturers, also compress data before it is saved. Therefore, these backup programs can also be used as offline compression programs.

Selecting A Compression Program

Which compression program you should use mainly depends on availability. For example, if you've just purchased a new PC that has DOS 6, you should probably use DoubleSpace. Or, if you're already using PC Tools, you probably won't find a compression program that outperforms Compress and Expand. However, we'll provide some guidelines you can use to determine which program is best for you.

1. If you don't have a lot of disk space and can't or don't want to move some of the data to diskettes, you must use data compression. However, if you can move some data onto floppy diskettes, you can probably solve your problem by simply making backups.

2. If you want to compress only certain types of files at certain times, you should consider using offline data compression. Therefore, you can determine what will be compressed and when it will be decompressed.

3. If you don't want to use data compression, but still want to increase the space on your hard drive, you may want to consider online data compression.

If you've decided to use online data compression, you still must choose the particular program you'll use.

1. If you've installed DOS 6, you should simply use DoubleSpace. Since you already have a compression program, you won't find a less-expensive alternative.

Introduction to Data Compression

Chapter One

2. If you're using an earlier version of DOS than Version 6, you could either upgrade to DOS 6 or purchase a separate online compressor, such as Stacker or DoubleDensity. Since a DOS upgrade isn't too expensive, this may be the most economical option. However, DoubleDensity is also affordable. This can be an alternative to upgrading older DOS versions.

3. You should use Stacker if data compression is extremely important to you. After all, this specialized program is equipped with functions that DoubleSpace lacks, such as special optimization tools and a Windows Tuning Interface.

Hardware and Software Requirements

The main purpose of online data compression is, obviously, to reduce the amount you must spend on additional hardware and software. In other words, it's intended to prevent you from having to invest in a larger and faster hard drive.

However, for online data compression to work effectively, certain hardware and software is needed.

Operating system

You shouldn't use a DOS version lower than 5.0; Version 6.0 or 6.2 is preferable. Older DOS versions cannot manage hard drives of more than 32 Meg directly. These versions must first divide such hard drives into separate partitions. For example, a 40 Meg hard drive, must be split into two disks with 20 Meg each, or perhaps one with 10 and the other with 30 Meg. However, as soon as you double the disk capacity, even a 20 Meg drive will turn into a 40 Meg drive, thus exceeding the 32 Meg limit. Therefore, the older DOS versions would require even this disk to be partitioned.

Introduction to Data Compression

Chapter One

Interfaces

If you're using an interface, such as Norton Commander, DOS Shell, or PC Tools, you can continue using your current version of the interface. Since compressed hard drives work just like normal drives, they don't cause any problems for these applications.

Windows

If you're using Windows, you should have Version 3.1. This is important not necessarily because of the data compression, but for all the other advantages this version offers over its predecessors. Also, the Stacker utilities only run starting with Windows 3.0. Another good reason to update from 3.0 to 3.1 is that this version includes TrueType fonts and an improved File Manager.

Processor

Data compression works with all types of processors. Theoretically, it's even possible to use data compression with an 8088 or 8086. However, as we mentioned, data compression slows down the overall system performance because it requires processor power.

Therefore, if you're already annoyed by your system's lack of speed, then adding a compression program will definitely increase your frustration. Also, if you're running Windows, you shouldn't be using anything less than a 386 processor with 4 Meg of RAM.

To achieve the best performance you need an 80486 or Pentium processor and at least 8 Meg of RAM.

Hard drive

One reason for using data compression is to avoid having to buy a new hard drive. However, it's not really financially viable to double the capacity of a 20 or 40 Meg hard drive. After all, compression programs cost almost as much as an entire hard drive.

Today you can get hard drives with 120 Meg for around $200, or about $1.60 per megabyte. If, however, you choose to double the capacity of a 40 Meg hard drive to 80 Meg using Stacker (the software version is available for around $100, you'll pay $2.50 per megabyte.

Introduction to Data Compression

Chapter One

The numbers speak for themselves. Data compression becomes truly affordable with large hard drives. For example, doubling a 120 megabyte drive to 240 megabytes costs about $1.20 per additional megabyte. Purchasing a comparable 240 megabyte hard drives will run about $340, roughly $2.80 per megabyte.

If you're planning on compressing not only rarely-used data, but all your files and programs, you should make sure that you're using a hard drive with fast access times (under 20 milliseconds). Otherwise, your system will slow down dramatically.

Chapter 2

Data Compression In Detail

Contents

Logical and Physical Drives 15

Partitions 16

RAM Drives 17

Compressed Volume Files (CVFs) 17

Host Drives 18

Compression Factor 18

Compression Ratios 20

Compression Speed 21

Fragmentation 22

Cross-linked File Clusters 23

Memory Types 23

Memory Management 25

Protecting Your Data 25

Data Compression In Detail

Chapter Two

Now that you know the basics of data compression, its advantages and disadvantages, possible dangers, and what type of programs are available, in this chapter we'll discuss online data compression in detail. You'll learn the specific terminology and techniques that are the basis for all compression programs, regardless of whether you're using DoubleSpace, Stacker, or DoubleDensity.

Logical and Physical Drives

Most PC users, even beginners, usually know how many floppy and hard disk drives are installed on their system. Also, most users know that the disk drives are addressed as A: and B:, and that the first hard drive is called C:. However, many users are surprised to discover that they can address a drive D: or even E: in a PC with only two floppy drives and one hard drive.

This is possible because DOS can use two kinds of disk drives, called logical and physical drives. Physical drives are the ones that are actually installed in your PC. In other words, these are the ones you can physically touch if you remove the case. These generally include one or two floppy disk drives, a hard drive, and in some cases a CD ROM drive. In addition to these physical drives, DOS is able to "pretend" that additional drives are installed. This can be useful in several ways:

1. It's common to set up RAM drives (see the following section) in the PC's memory for temporarily storing data. In this case, therefore, the PC's main memory is used to simulate a disk drive. This RAM drive will be addressed as C: if the system doesn't have a hard drive; otherwise it's addressed with D: (or the next available drive if a drive D: exists).

Data Compression In Detail

Chapter Two

2. Older DOS versions could manage only hard drives with up to 32 Meg of disk space. Anyone with a disk with more than 32 Meg was forced to divide the disk into two or more drives, or partitions (see the following section). Today it is sometimes still useful to partition extremely large hard drives into several drives, which are then addressed with D:, E:, etc. This makes it easier to organize a large amount of different files.

3. Within networks, it's possible to make drives and directories of certain PCs available to other users on the network. To permit access to these remote files, the directories that are being accessed receive names that act like disk drive IDs. Therefore, the directory "C:\TEXTS" on a user's PC might be identified as drive E: from within the network.

4. Finally, online compression programs let you compress data on only part of your hard drive. The compressed portion then receives its own drive letter, for example D:.

Now you know of several situations in which pseudo disk drives are used in addition to installed physical drives. These pseudo-drives are called logical drives, since they exist within the PC's logical system, but not the physical world.

Partitions

Partitions are a way of using logical drives. Before Version 4.0 of DOS, partitions were needed whenever hard drives with more than 32 Meg were used. Partitions are also used whenever a dual-boot system (a PC with two operating systems, such as DOS and OS/2) is set up.

Under DOS, partitions are created using the FDISK program (see Chapter 3), which is also used to manage the partitions that are created. Each partition receives one of the available drive letters, usually starting with D:. The compressed drive doesn't require its own partition, since it's used as an oversized hidden file.

Data Compression In Detail

Chapter Two

RAM Drives

RAM or virtual drives are also logical drives, except that they exist in a portion of your PC's main memory. Before all PCs were equipped with a hard drive, virtual drives provided an effective way to make temporarily-needed files available quickly or even to fully simulate a second drive. However, today virtual drives are rarely used.

RAM drives are installed in the CONFIG.SYS file using one of the device drivers, VDISK.SYS or RAMDRIVE.SYS. If a hard drive isn't installed, they receive the drive letter C:; otherwise, D: is used. A portion of the system's RAM, which can be freely selected, will then be used just like a drive.

However, like all data stored in RAM, the information in the virtual drive will be lost once the PC is switched off or power is lost. Therefore, RAM drives are useful only for temporary files, or for data that will be copied to a diskette or the hard drive. However, the data stored on (in) the RAM drive are accessed much faster than on a physical disk. (This increase in speed isn't as significant if a fast hard drive is used.)

Compressed Volume Files (CVFs)

As we mentioned, compressed drives aren't implemented as separate partitions. Instead, they are used as special files, called Compressed Volume Files (CVFs). These are extremely large files containing the entire compressed drive. To prevent these drive files from being deleted accidentally, their hidden attribute is set, so they are invisible within the DOS environment.

However, there is still the danger that these files might be deleted with utility programs such as Norton Utilities or PC Tools. Therefore, you must be extremely careful when deleting files on the drive that contains the CVF. You should first back up the files on the compressed drive so you won't lose your compressed data if the wrong file is deleted.

Data Compression In Detail

Chapter Two

Instead of gradually increasing in size as you store more data in it, the CVF is already at full size when you first install it on your drive. In other words, if you compress 20 Meg of your hard drive, then the CVF will be 20 Meg immediately upon installation, thus reducing the remaining space on the hard drive by 20 Meg. However, you'll have an additional 40 Meg of storage space on your compressed drive.

Host Drives

Host drives are the physical drives on which the CVFs for the compressed drives are located. Therefore, host drives are either partially or completely compressed themselves.

The directory of the host drive will, in turn, contain the hidden CVF files for the compressed drive.

Compression Factor

Most compression programs claim to have various compression factors. This occurs because all users want to get as much space as possible out of their hard drive. This factor indicates by what percentage the files are compressed and, therefore, by what percentage the compression increases the available disk space.

Also, many advertisements for compression programs refer to the hard drive compression as hard drive "doubling". This is misleading because it implies that the hard drive capacity will be increased by at least 100 percent. However, that's only partially true.

As you've probably realized, different types of files can be compressed only by varying degrees (more about this in the next section). Generally, graphic files have a higher rate of compression than application files, for example.

Data Compression In Detail

Chapter Two

Therefore, it's only possible to provide a true and reliable compression factor once the compressed drive has been completely filled with data. Only then can you compare the data's compressed and uncompressed size, resulting in a percentage.

While the compressed drive doesn't contain any data, you can only guess at the compression factor. This guess must be based on experience and the assumption that the data stored on the drive will consist of a certain combination of application, text, spreadsheet, database, and graphic files. It's this estimated average value that's used to make the claim about doubling the hard drive capacity.

So you should be wary of the indicated amount of remaining free disk space on a compressed drive. Although compression programs will continually recalculate the projected compression factor, these indications are still only estimates. After all, if you initially save a lot of graphic files the program will obtain a high compression factor.

Based on this factor, the compression program will indicate that a corresponding amount of megabytes of compressed disk space are still available. Then if you start saving program files, this indicated figure will no longer be valid. If you compress original program diskettes (which are already compressed) on a compressed drive in order to create backup copies, the compression factor will drop to below 1.1 or 10 percent.

Ultimately, you'll be able to determine the actual compression factor that you'll obtain by carefully selecting what you compress. If you avoid compressing files that can't really be compressed much further, you'll make the most of your compressed drive.

The advertised doubling of hard drive capacity is deceptive and applicable only under the right circumstances. However, under ideal circumstances you may actually achieve higher compression factors as well.

DoubleSpace lets you specify the compression factor manually, which is misleading. However, this doesn't let you determine the density with which DoubleSpace actually packs your data. Instead, this function lets you determine the estimated compression factor yourself and, therefore, DOS' indication of free/used disk space.

20　　Data Compression In Detail

Chapter Two

So, if you know that you'll be compressing only a certain type of file, then you'll be able to obtain a more accurate estimate of the free disk space by adjusting the estimated compression factor accordingly. However, that's all you can do with this function.

When Stacker allows you to choose between higher and lower compression levels, you're actually specifying the intensity of compression. The program can operate faster by compressing less intensely. However, even with a maximum compression intensity, Stacker still won't be able to compress a program file to half the size of its original.

Compression Ratios

As we mentioned above, different types of files can be compressed to varying degrees. Obviously, you want to gain as much disk space as possible by using data compression. However, some files are suitable for compression.

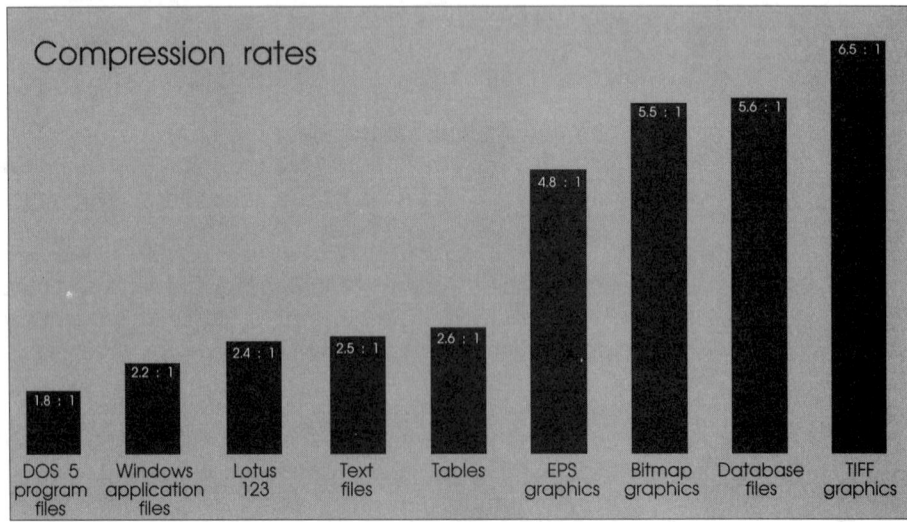

Different compression rates

Data Compression In Detail

Chapter Two

As the graph shows, compressing program files isn't worthwhile. However, you can achieve high compression rates with graphics of all kinds and databases which use fixed field lengths, such as dBase. Here the compressed file can even be seven times smaller than its original.

Compression Speed

Compression speed is just as important as the compression factor. After all, the best compression rate is useless if it takes forever to compress or uncompress a file. Unfortunately, it's impossible to provide accurate figures on compression speed. Consider the following factors:

- Since calculations are involved, the processor affects the compression speed.

- The hard drive affects the compression speed almost as much, since data is read and written.

- A coprocessor may increase the compression speed, because at least Stacker uses this mathematical assistant. You can even get an entire coprocessor board for Stacker, which will increase the working speed.

- The amount of available RAM and the performance of the memory chips themselves will also affect the compression speed, since all of the data flows through RAM. The actual compression software can be stored in extended memory.

Here's an actual example of how compression speed can be affected. On our PC (486 DX, 33 MHz with local bus, 8 Meg of RAM, 250 Meg hard drive), we set up a 100 Meg as a compressed drive and stored primarily text files on this drive.

Even if you're working under Windows, you'll find that compressed text files will load and save just as fast as their non-compressed counterparts. In any case, it's impossible to detect a real difference between the two.

Data Compression In Detail

Chapter Two

With Stacker, it's possible to select between higher speed and higher compression through its Fine-Tuning feature. DoubleSpace doesn't let you do this. Therefore, any Stacker users who aren't satisfied with its performance have the option of increasing its speed by sacrificing some disk space.

Fragmentation

MS-DOS stores files on the hard drive in clusters, with sizes ranging from 512 bytes to several kilobytes. This cluster arrangement allows files to be read more quickly and to be managed more easily. However, this arrangement also creates some problems.

Files under 512 bytes, for example, still occupy an entire 512-byte cluster. The rest of the cluster isn't used. Larger files occupy several clusters and the last cluster is normally only partially used. However, there is also a much more significant problem: If a file is larger than one cluster, but not enough adjacent clusters are available to store the file contiguously, the file is stored in segments at different disk locations. So, the file is scattered, or fragmented, across the disk.

This fragmentation doesn't present an immediate problem, because DOS can easily find the file's respective parts again, reassemble them when it reads the file, and put them back in the correct place when it writes the file. However, ultimately this fragmentation leads to increased read and write times. Also, fragmentation increases the chances that a cluster will actually be lost (see the "Cross-linked File Clusters" section in this chapter). This, in turn, decreases data security.

However, it's possible to reverse the effects of fragmentation by using special defragmentation utilities. Up to DOS Version 5.0, users had to use applications such as PC Tools or Norton Utilities, since only these supplementary programs were actually equipped with a defragmenter. However starting with DOS 6.0, a basic version of Norton's DEFRAG has been included with DOS. We'll discuss this program in detail in Chapter 3.

Data Compression In Detail

Chapter Two

Cross-linked File Clusters

Cross-linked file clusters are another problem associated with the use of clusters. Although these clusters contain data, they cannot be assigned to any particular file. In other words, they contain garbage data.

This data accumulates mainly during system crashes. According to the Microsoft manual, most of this data stems from temporary files, such as the ones used by applications to back up new documents that haven't been saved yet. However, as most PC users eventually realize, cross-linked file clusters quickly accumulate even without system crashes.

If you're using MS-DOS 6.2, use SCANDISK to repair disk problems. It can repair problems which are not fixed by CHKDSK.

To reassemble these cross-linked file clusters in new files, use the DOS utility CHKDSK, which is included in most DOS versions. These files can then be deleted or used in some other way. (We'll discuss CHKDSK in more detail in Chapter 3.)

Memory Types

The management of compressed hard drives even affects how your PC's memory is used. The use of the compression program requires a special driver, which intercepts all read/write operations. In order for the driver to do this, it must be installed as a memory-resident program within your computer's main memory.

To be able to use your PC's RAM as effectively as possible, you should be familiar with the different memory types:

Data Compression In Detail

Chapter Two

Conventional memory	0-640K
Upper memory	640K to 1 Meg
High memory	1 Meg to 1088K
Extended memory	>1 Meg
Expanded memory	>1 Meg

Conventional memory ranges from 0 to 640K and represents the address range that is addressable directly by DOS, even in its older versions. The DOS system kernels are usually stored within this range, and this is also where all applications are executed. The majority of program data are also stored within Conventional memory. Therefore, you should always place everything that doesn't absolutely have to be in Conventional memory somewhere else, so that applications and their data have as much memory as possible.

However, you can move this data to a different location only if your PC has more than 640K of RAM. Since the 80286 was introduced, a minimum of 1 Meg of RAM has been standard. Because of this, now Upper memory (from 640K to 1 Meg) is available.

Upper memory is already used to store screen data, at least when the video card doesn't have enough memory on its own. However, even then, there's plenty of extra room in Upper memory. Starting with Version 4.0, DOS can store some of its system files within this address range. Most of the system drivers, for example, can be copied into upper memory. This also includes the driver for the hard drive duplicators.

If your system has more than 1 Meg of RAM, you'll be able to use the first 64K above the 1 Meg limit as High memory. This memory can also be used to store system drivers and various parts of DOS.

Finally, under Windows you can use the region above 1 Meg for applications and data. This additional memory range is called Extended memory. This way, RAM sizes of 4 Meg and more can be used under Windows.

Data Compression In Detail

Chapter Two

However, memory above 1 Meg can also be accessed under DOS if it's used as Expanded memory. With this method, portions of the memory above 1 Meg are superimposed in the lower memory region just like windows or separate pages, and are thus made available to DOS. If other data or programs are needed, the required memory segment is shown through the memory window (a process known as paging).

Memory Management

DOS is responsible for managing the PC's memory. It uses several tools to do this. The different memory management programs (for Expanded memory, for example) are installed in your CONFIG.SYS and AUTOEXEC.BAT files. Using MEM (starting with DOS 4.0), you can check the amount of available and used memory. Using MEMMAKER (starting with DOS 6.0), you can automatically optimize your system's memory organization.

We'll discuss memory optimization in detail in the chapters on DoubleSpace and Stacker. The DOS programs MEM and MEMMAKER are discussed in the "MEM and MEMMAKER" section in Chapter 3. We'll focus on the settings that are important to hard drive compression programs.

Protecting Your Data

Data security is extremely important to data and disk compression. Remember that the data density and, therefore, the information density that's obtained is considerably higher than on normal drives. So, even the smallest problem can result in a large loss of data.

Viruses, power outages, and headcrashes (when the read/write heads impact the disk surface) are especially dangerous. Your best protection against viruses is a regular virus check, which should include your

Data Compression In Detail

Chapter Two

compressed drive. Before using a memory-resident virus checker, be sure that it's compatible with the compressed drive (thoroughly check the documentation and Readme files for the software that you're using).

If a power outage occurs, perform a CHKDSK or SCANDISK on your compressed disk to ensure that it wasn't damaged.

Headcrashes are very dangerous for compressed hard drives. Since you cannot tell when a headcrash occurs, you'll probably realize one has occurred when you discover that a certain file will no longer load, or your drive seems to be stuck.

To detect hard drive damage as early as possible, you should perform a surface scan using the PC Tools for Windows Optimizer or PC Tools for DOS COMPRESS. This checks the readability of your hard drive sectors. Any sectors that cannot be read (i.e., damaged sectors) are locked from further access, which prevents future data loss. Norton Utilities also provides a similar function.

The SCANDISK utility of MS-DOS 6.2 also can scan the surface of a disk for defects or errors.

You should regularly back up your compressed drive. Remember, since an average of twice the data of a normal disk is stored on your compressed drive, any data loss will be that much worse. Therefore, it's extremely important that you make backup copies.

Starting with DOS 6.2, DoubleSpace uses the DoubleGuard safety system. Working in the background, DoubleGuard checks whether the data that will be written on the compressed drive is acceptable.

To do this, DoubleGuard evaluates the data's technical consistency, since the content can't really be controlled. It's automatically activated when DoubleSpace is installed, and doesn't affect the operation of DoubleSpace. Although it's possible to deactivate DoubleGuard from the DOS environment, this isn't necessary.

CHAPTER 3

Before Compressing Your Hard Drive

Contents

FDISK 29

FORMAT 34

CHKDSK 36

DEFRAG 37

BACKUP 39

MEM and MEMMAKER 70

ScanDisk (DOS 6.2 and above) 78

Before Compressing Your Hard Drive

Chapter Three

Before installing a compressed hard drive on your system with DoubleSpace, Stacker, or DoubleDensity, you must be familiar with the DOS utility programs for hard drive and memory management. Without an understanding of these programs, usually it's impossible to compress your hard drive.

> **Note**
>
> Any information in this book about DOS refers to Version 6.2. It's impossible to include information on all versions of DOS. If you need additional help, refer to your DOS manual or to DOS 6 Complete by Abacus.

For example, before compressing your hard drive, you must partition it using FDISK, format it with FORMAT, and check for errors using CHKDSK.

You should also defragment your hard drive with DEFRAG and secure your data with BACKUP. Use MEM to analyze how conventional memory is organized and MEMMAKER to optimize conventional memory.

FDISK

As we mentioned in Chapter 1, you should use a version of DOS that can directly manage hard drives with more than 32 Meg of disk space. Versions 4.0, 4.1, 5.0 and 6 have this capability. Otherwise, you must split up the hard drives into several partitions and you might even have to partition the compressed drives themselves. Since this is very complicated, we recommend updating your version of DOS.

Be sure that you can address your hard drive as a single partition and drive. Remember the compression process already divides your hard drive into two drives. Therefore, it's useless to add any extra, unnecessary partitions.

Before Compressing Your Hard Drive

Chapter Three

If you purchased your computer brand new and have DOS 4.0 or above, your hard drive is probably already set up as one partition. If this is the case, you don't have to worry about performing the following procedure.

However, if you've been working with several partitions and logical drives, you must remove these partitions and drives and then install one large new partition. To do this, use the FDISK program.

> **Warning**
> Before deleting partitions and drives, back up the data on your entire hard drive. Refer to the "BACKUP" section in this chapter for more information on backing up data.

When you delete partitions, you'll lose all the data on that partition. Since you must also temporarily delete the primary DOS partition before setting up the entire hard drive as a single partition, you must include the core of the system in your backup.

Always have a boot diskette available so you can start your system from a diskette after partitioning. Include your backup program on this start diskette, so you can copy back the data from the backup to your new partitioned hard drive. Also, ensure the Format utility program is on your boot diskette, so you can also format your new hard drive. We'll discuss how to create a boot diskette in the next section.

> **Note**
> If you've been working with partitions of the DiskManager, SpeedStor, Priam, or Everex programs, you cannot remove these partitions with FDISK. Instead, you must use the special software accompanying these programs.

Activate FDISK from DOS by entering:

```
FDISK Enter
```

The startup screen of the program appears with the **Main** menu.

Before Compressing Your Hard Drive

Chapter Three

```
                    MS-DOS Version 6
                 Fixed Disk Setup Program
              (C)Copyright Microsoft Corp. 1983 - 1993

                        FDISK Options

   Current fixed disk drive: 1

   Choose one of the following:

   1. Create DOS partition or Logical DOS Drive
   2. Set active partition
   3. Delete partition or Logical DOS Drive
   4. Display partition information


   Enter choice: [1]


   WARNING! No partitions are set active - disk 1 is not startable unless
   a partition is set active


   Press Esc to exit FDISK
```

FDISK Main menu

Note

If your system has more than one physical hard drive, FDISK automatically processes the first hard drive, C:. To run FDISK on other hard drives, select Option 5 and enter the number for the other hard drive (2=D, 3=E, etc.)

Choose Option 4 to determine the number of partitions into which your hard drive is divided. A screen appears displaying the partition information.

Before Compressing Your Hard Drive

Chapter Three

```
                    Display Partition Information
Current fixed disk drive: 1

Partition  Status    Type      Volume Label  Mbytes   System    Usage
C: 1                 PRI DOS                 60       UNKNOWN   50%
   2                 EXT DOS                 59                 50%


Total disk space is  119 Mbytes (1 Mbyte = 1048576 bytes)


The Extended DOS Partition contains Logical DOS Drives.
Do you want to display the logical drive information (Y/N)......?[Y]




Press Esc to return to FDISK Options
```

Partition information

Display the information about the logical DOS drives and then press (Esc) to quit. Now you know how many drives and partitions are set up on your hard drive.

If you have a non-DOS partition, such as an OS/2 partition, and you won't need it in the future, choose Option 3 to delete this partition. Now the **Delete** menu appears.

Before Compressing Your Hard Drive

Chapter Three

```
                Delete DOS Partition or Logical DOS Drive

Current fixed disk drive: 1

Choose one of the following:

1.  Delete Primary DOS Partition
2.  Delete Extended DOS Partition
3.  Delete Logical DOS Drive(s) in the Extended DOS Partition
4.  Delete Non-DOS Partition



Enter choice: [ ]




Press Esc to return to FDISK Options
```

Delete menu

To remove the non-DOS partition, choose Option 4 from the **Delete** menu. A security prompt appears.

Type the number of the partition you want to delete and press [Enter] to confirm your choice. Press [Y] to delete the partition.

Deleting logical DOS drives and extended DOS partitions is similar. Choose Option 3 in the **Main** menu, then in the **Delete** menu choose the partition or drive type you want deleted. Finally, delete the primary DOS partition, which also contains the start information for your PC. Now you've eliminated all partitions and drives and you can start re-installing your hard drive.

First create your new primary DOS partition. Choose Option 1 in the **Main** menu of FDISK. The **Create** menu appears.

Before Compressing Your Hard Drive

Chapter Three

```
              Create DOS Partition or Logical DOS Drive

Current fixed disk drive: 1

Choose one of the following:

1. Create Primary DOS Partition
2. Create Extended DOS Partition
3. Create Logical DOS Drive(s) in the Extended DOS Partition




Enter choice: [1]




Press Esc to return to FDISK Options
```

Create menu

Before proceeding with the next step, be sure you have prepared a boot diskette and made a backup of your files. You are about to lose all data on your hard drive. If you do not know how to create a boot diskette, refer to the next section, your DOS users manual or *DOS 6 Complete* from Abacus. Instructions for creating a backup of your hard disk are included in another section of this chapter.

In this menu, choose Option 1 to create the primary DOS partition. A security prompt appears. Confirm the prompt with [Y] since you want the new partition to include the entire hard drive. After creating the primary partition, your system will reboot. Place your prepared boot diskette into drive A:.

FORMAT

You still must format your newly partitioned hard drive. After restarting your PC, enter the following command line when the DOS prompt appears:

Before Compressing Your Hard Drive

Chapter Three

```
A:FORMAT C: /S [Enter]
```

Answer the security prompt with [Y]. This command line activates the format program on the diskette you inserted in drive A:. This program formats your hard drive (C:) and provides the system files (/s). Once the program finishes, you can restart your system from the hard drive.

Then you must copy back your backup data to the hard drive. (For more information, refer to the "BACKUP" section in this chapter.)

Creating a boot diskette

You can also use FORMAT to format a boot diskette. From the hard drive, use the following procedure:

- Insert a diskette in drive A:

- Enter the following command:

    ```
    FORMAT A: /S [Enter]
    ```

Confirm the security prompt with [Y].

- Select **Copy** to copy your backup program, as well as the format program, to the diskette. Add other useful DOS utility programs.

- Create a CONFIG.SYS and AUTOEXEC.BAT file for the boot diskette. These files run your system.

The following is an example of a CONFIG.SYS file:

```
BUFFERS=30,0
FILES=40
LASTDRIVE=Z
FCBS=16,8
BREAK ON
SHELL=a:\COMMAND.COM /P /E:1024
STACKS=9,256
```

Here's an example of an AUTOEXEC.BAT file:

Before Compressing Your Hard Drive

Chapter Three

```
@ECHO OFF
PROMPT $p$g
```

Along with these system files, your boot diskette should also include the following files:

- MSDOS.SYS
- IO.SYS
- COMMAND.COM

These files are copied automatically by using the /s switch of the FORMAT command. MSDOS.SYS and IO.SYS are hidden system files and cannot be seen by entering DIR.

CHKDSK

Use CHKDSK to locate cross-linked file clusters. (These are clusters that are created during system crashes or power outages.) Then you can either display these file remnants and use them in some other way or simply delete them.

Use the following command line at the DOS prompt to activate CHKDSK:

CHKDSK /f [Enter]

Note

Always run CHKDSK to check your hard drive for cross-linked file clusters before defragmenting it. Also, you must run CHKDSK before installing a compressed drive.

The /f switch not only makes certain the command checks the hard drive for errors, but also places cross-linked file clusters in files with the .CHK extension.

If there are cross-linked file clusters, CHKDSK writes them to the root directory of the hard drive in files with names such as FILE0001.CHK,

Before Compressing Your Hard Drive

Chapter Three

FILE0002.CHK, etc. Then you can display each file in a text editor to determine which CHK files still contain useful information. This is especially helpful for text files.

Delete the CHK files you don't need with ERASE or DELETE.

DEFRAG

Before installing your compressed drive, defragment the hard drive. If you're using DOS 6.0 or DOS 6.2, you can use the DEFRAG utility program. If you have an older version of DOS, you must use PC Tools or Norton Utilities; each of these has its own defragmenting tool. In this section we'll discuss how the DOS defragmenting program works. For information about PC Tools or Norton Utilities, refer to your user's manual.

Activate DEFRAG from the DOS prompt by entering the following command line:

DEFRAG [Enter]

The following start screen appears, allowing you to select the drive to be optimized.

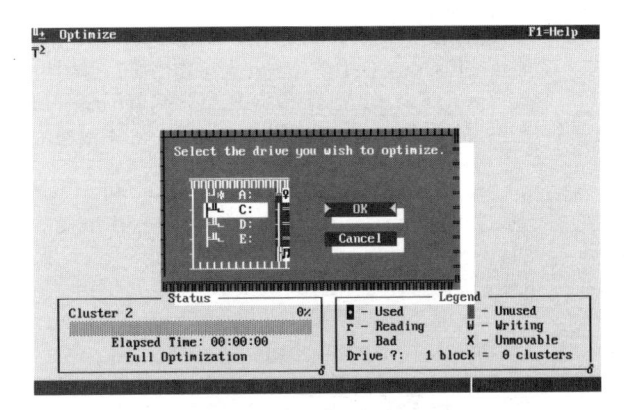

Selecting the drive to be defragmented

38 Before Compressing Your Hard Drive

Chapter Three

Use the cursor keys to select the desired drive and then press Enter.

DEFRAG checks your hard drive for fragmented files. At the end, the program displays a suggestion.

DEFRAG suggests what you should do

You should follow DEFRAG's recommendation. To do this, simply press Enter to begin optimization.

First the program rewrites the directories and DEFRAG begins undoing (breaking up) the fragmentation. To do this, the program writes files to new clusters. In the map of the hard drive that appears on the screen, "W" refers to the clusters DEFRAG is writing, while "r" indicates the clusters DEFRAG is reading. The defragmented clusters appear in yellow.

The Status area is located in the lower-left corner of the screen. In this area, you can see which cluster the program is reading, how much time has elapsed, and what percentage of defragmenting is completed. After DEFRAG finishes optimizing, it displays the message "Finished Condensing." Click OK to quit. A new prompt appears, asking you to choose your next option.

Click the Exit DEFRAG button to exit the defragmentation program.

Before Compressing Your Hard Drive

Chapter Three

BACKUP

You must make backup copies of your data to protect it. With backup copies, you can recover the data you lose because of hard drive defects, head crashes, system crashes, and power failures. Therefore, back up your important data and programs regularly. Obviously, backups are especially important on compressed hard drives because they contain much more data than normal drives.

DOS contains a special backup program. In DOS versions up to 5.0, this program is called BACKUP and RESTORE. Starting with Version 6.0, the program is called MSBACKUP and is available as both a DOS and a Windows version. We'll briefly describe all three backup programs.

Remember, you should perform a complete backup before installing the compression software. If you must also repartition the hard drive, backing up your data is an absolute necessity.

MSBACKUP for DOS

To make a backup copy with MSBACKUP for DOS, start the program from the DOS prompt by entering the following

```
MSBACKUP  Enter
```

or selecting "Backup Fixed Disk" from the Disk Utilities group in the DOS Shell. The **Main** menu of the backup program appears.

Before Compressing Your Hard Drive

Chapter Three

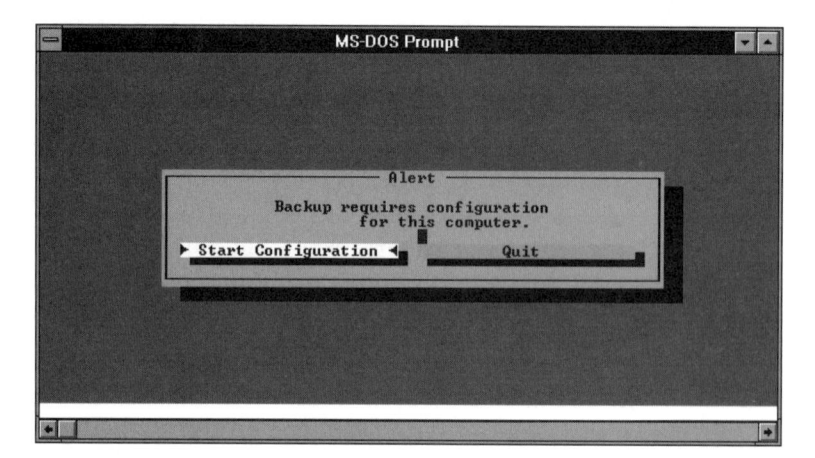

The Backup Main menu

Click the (Backup) button. The Backup screen appears.

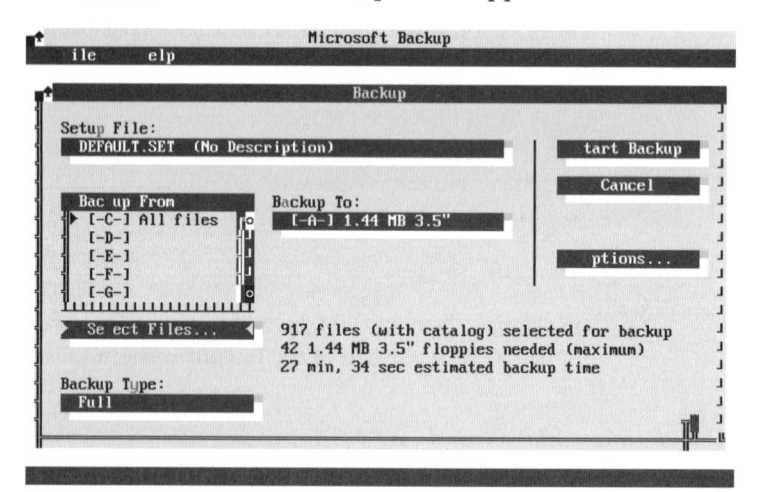

The Backup screen

"Setup File:"

Specifies the configuration file, in which settings such as backup drives, speed, mouse, and screen settings are stored. Theoretically, you could be working with several setup files and load a different setup file here.

Before Compressing Your Hard Drive

Chapter Three

"Backup To:"

Specifies the disk drive on which you want to create the backups. You should choose the drive with the highest capacity.

"Backup From:"

Specifies the hard drive from which you want to make a backup. Usually this will be drive C:.

Click [Select Files] to determine which files will be included in the backup. The "Select Backup Files" dialog box appears.

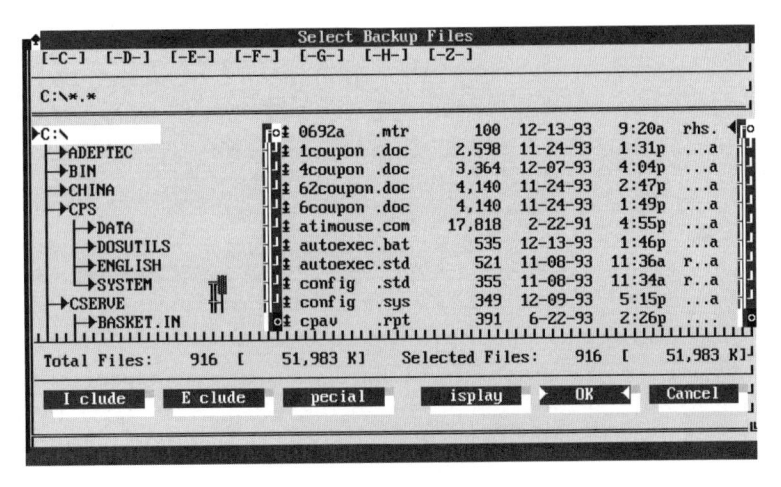

Selecting backup files

There are several ways you can select files for the backup:

1. Manual Selection:
   In the directory tree, move to the directory that you want to back up. To save all the files of this directory, press the [Spacebar] or double-click to select the entire directory. In the file list on the right, a checkmark appears in front of all the selected files.

Before Compressing Your Hard Drive

Chapter Three

You can also select individual files in the file list. To cancel a selection, click the right mouse button. File selection works like a toggle switch. This means that by using exactly the same methods, you can unselect any file that is currently selected.

Click [Display] to customize the file list.

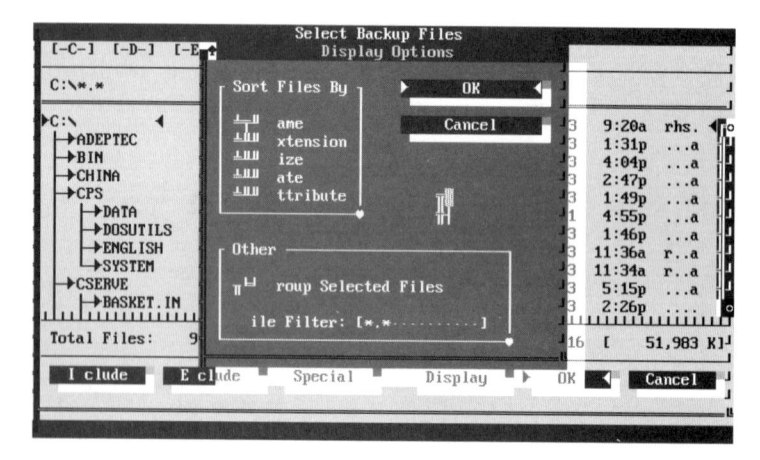

Display options

You can sort files in the list by name, extension, size, date, and attribute. It's also possible to limit the files to be displayed by using the "File Filter" text box. "Group Selected Files" lets you place the selected files of a directory at the beginning of the file list.

2. Include:
   Click the [Include] button to determine which files to include in the backup.

Before Compressing Your Hard Drive

Chapter Three

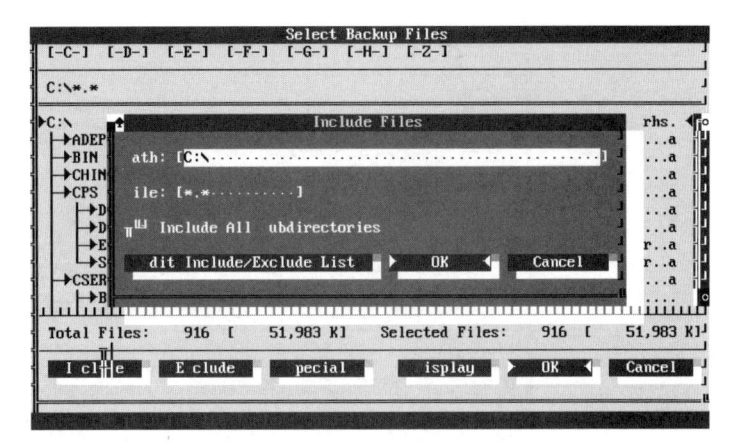

Include dialog box

Specify the path you want to include in the backup and, if you don't want to back up the complete directory, type a filename after "File." "Include All Subdirectories" lets you include the subdirectories of the selected directory in the backup.

Click [OK] to confirm the information entered in this dialog box. A checkmark appears before the filenames of all the files you selected.

3. Exclude:
   Click the [Exclude] button to exclude specific groups of files from a backup.

Before Compressing Your Hard Drive

Chapter Three

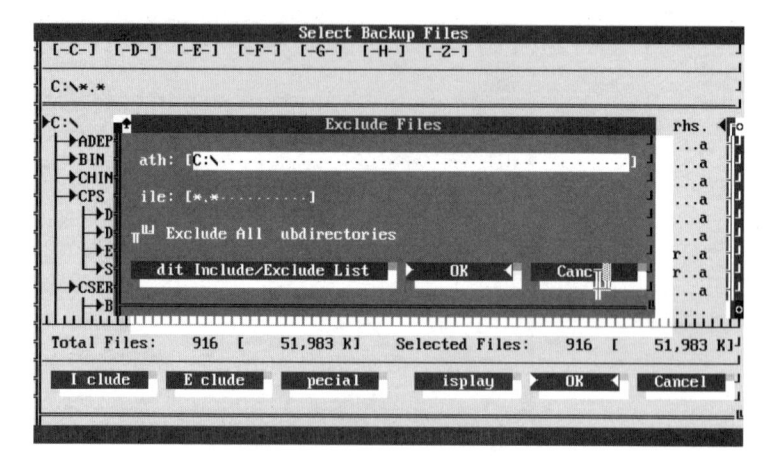

Exclude dialog box

Enter a path and a filename, as you did with "Include" and then confirm by choosing [OK].

4. Editing Exclude and Include information:
   You can revise the file lists created by "Include" and "Exclude." To do this, click either [Include] or [Exclude] and then choose the [Edit Include/Exclude List] button. The "Edit Include/Exclude List" dialog box appears.

Before Compressing Your Hard Drive

Chapter Three

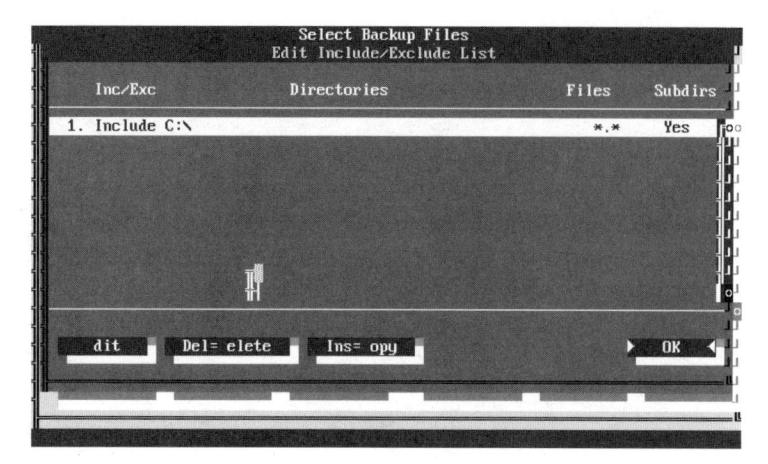

Editing the selection list

This dialog box contains all the entries you have made so far. Select an entry and click:

[Edit] to change the entry

[Del=Delete] to delete the entry

[Ins=Copy] to copy the entry and use it as a basis for an entry you modified with "Edit."

Click [OK] when you finish editing the list.

5. Special Entries:
The [Special] button lets you select files of a specific date range and exclude files with specific attributes.

Before Compressing Your Hard Drive

Chapter Three

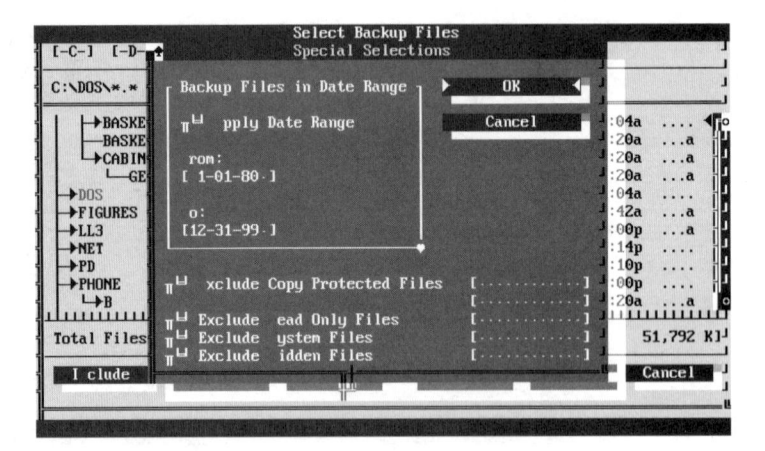

Special selections

"Backup Files in Date Range"

Lets you back up files between the dates specified in the "From:" and "To:" text boxes.

"Exclude Copy Protected Files"

Excludes the files that you enter in the five text boxes at the lower-right corner of the dialog box. This is a special option for program files that are copy protected.

"Exclude Read Only Files"

Excludes read only files from the backup.

"Exclude System Files"

Excludes system files from the backup. For example, it excludes IO.SYS and MSDOS.SYS.

"Exclude Hidden Files"

Excludes hidden files from the backup. For example, it excludes the IO.SYS and MSDOS.SYS files.

Before Compressing Your Hard Drive

Chapter Three

Click [OK] until you return to the Backup screen. After selecting the data for your backup, you can also choose backup options. Click the [Options] button.

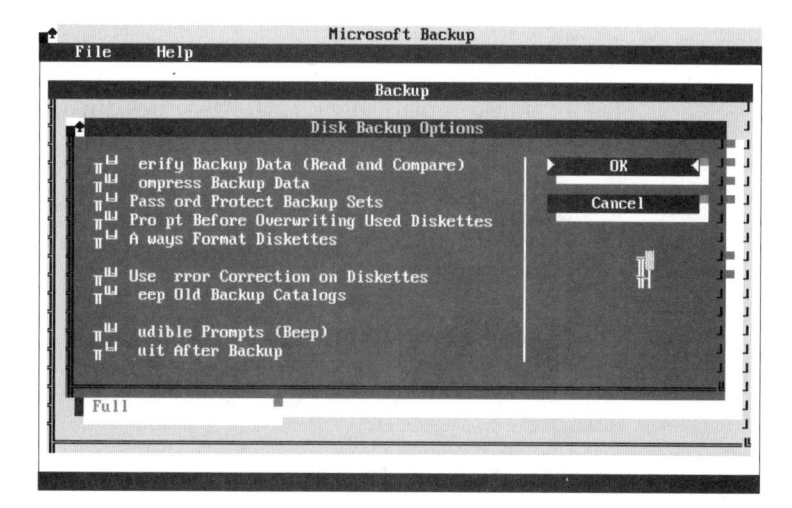

Backup options

The following is an overview of the options:

"Verify Backup Data (Read and Compare)"

This option verifies the data copied in the backup is correct. If you activate this check box, you don't have to compare the backup data and the original yourself. However, your backup will take longer.

"Compress Backup Data"

This option reduces the amount of disk space required for the backup data on the diskettes. This option reduces the amount of "disk swapping" (taking diskettes in and out of the drive) required during a backup.

"Password Protect Backup Sets"

This option protects your backup copies with a password.

Before Compressing Your Hard Drive

Chapter Three

"Prompt Before Overwriting Used Diskettes"

This option displays a security prompt before overwriting files from a previous backup.

"Always Format Diskettes"

This option automatically formats diskettes during the backup.

"Use Error Correction on Diskettes"

Increases data security through EEC, a correction procedure that RESTORE is able to use to copy back backup data stored in defective clusters on the diskette.

"Keep Old Backup Catalogs"

Lets you save the old backup catalog (list of all the backup files) on the hard drive.

"Audible Prompts (Beep)"

This option causes the computer to beep when you must insert a new diskette or perform some other activity during the backup.

"Quit After Backup"

This option closes the backup program when you're finished performing the backup.

Confirm the settings you've chosen by clicking [OK]. You return to the Backup screen. Now you must determine the type of backup.

Before Compressing Your Hard Drive

Chapter Three

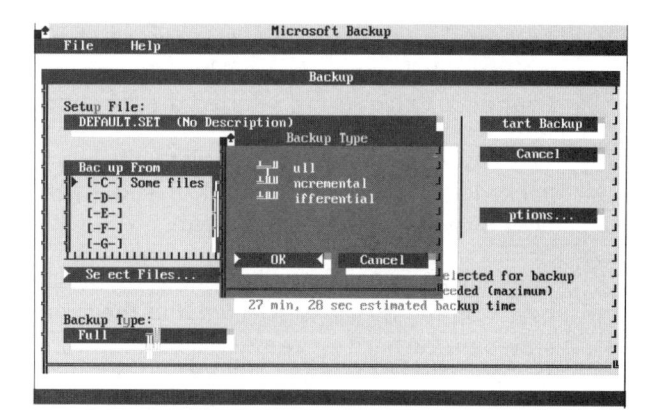

Selecting the backup method

You can choose from three backup methods:

Full

Backs up all selected files in sequence up to a contiguous disk set.

Incremental

Backs up only the selected files that have been changed or added since the last backup. An incremental backup adds to older backups (Full and Incremental) and doesn't overwrite any files. To completely restore your files, you must use the original Full backup and all incremental backups. You can perform any number of incremental backups.

Differential

Also backs up only new files and files that have been changed since the last backup, but a differential backup adds to older backups and also overwrites older versions of backup files.

You're probably wondering which backup method you should use. Your first backup should always be a full backup; otherwise, you'll never have all the necessary data together. You can use the incremental method for your daily backups. However, be sure to perform a full backup once a week. You could also add to your initial full backup by doing incremental

Before Compressing Your Hard Drive

Chapter Three

backups, but then you don't necessarily have to perform a full backup every week. Instead, do a full backup once a month, just to keep track of your data. Once you've selected the appropriate method, click OK.

The "Backup" dialog box displays the number of files that are being backed up, the number of blank diskettes you'll need for the backup, and how long the backup should take.

Now click Start Backup. First, the program creates the backup catalog, based on the files you selected and the type of backup. This catalog is stored on the hard drive and is used to restore files with RESTORE. Now the actual backup process starts. The program prompts you to insert diskettes. Be sure to label and number each blank diskette before using it.

During the backup, the program provides information about which diskettes are being accessed, which files are being copied, etc. Simply follow the instructions on the screen and exit the program when the backup is complete.

Restoring data

Eventually, you'll want to copy back the data from the backup to your hard drive. This process is called "restoring." To restore a backup, start the backup program by entering the following from the DOS prompt:

```
MSBACKUP Enter
```

In the DOS Shell, select the "MSBackup" entry in the "Disk Utilities" group. In the Main menu of MSBACKUP, select Restore. The "Restore" screen appears:

Before Compressing Your Hard Drive

Chapter Three

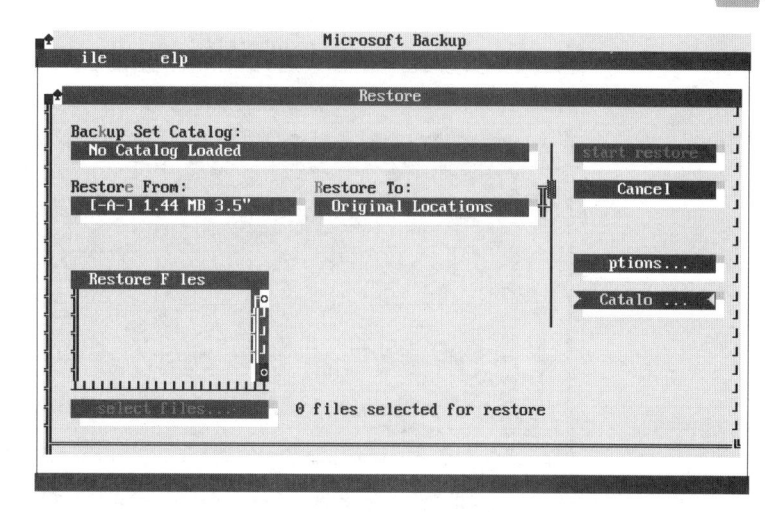

Restore screen

Follow these steps to restore your backup data:

1. Choose a backup catalog from which you can select the files you want to restore. You should have the catalog files of your last full backup and all subsequent differential and incremental backups as backup sets.

   If you don't, for example, because the catalog files on the hard drive have also been deleted, you must create a catalog file from the backup before doing anything else.

   To do this, insert the first backup diskette and then click [Catalog...].

Before Compressing Your Hard Drive

Chapter Three

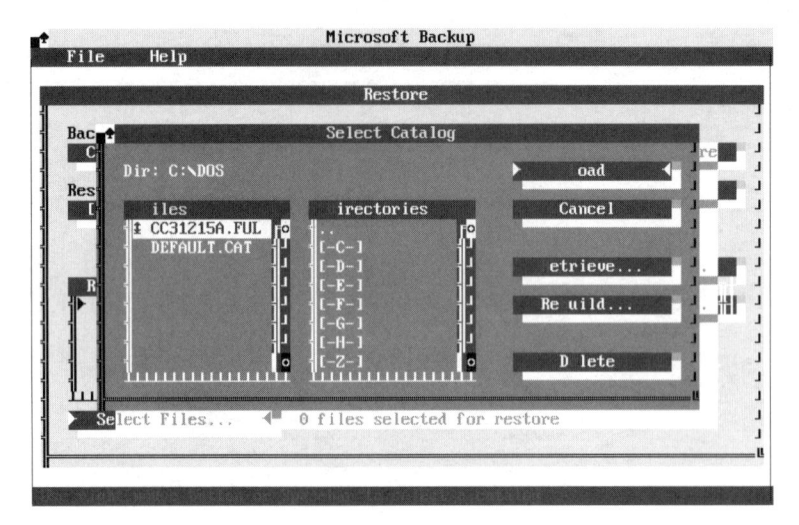

Selecting a catalog

Click [Retrieve...] and choose the backup drive. The program then reads in the catalog from the drive you selected. If this won't work, for example because the first backup diskette is damaged, click the [Rebuild...] button. BACKUP then creates a catalog file from the backup. If there is a catalog file on a different drive, you can find and select it in the "Files" and "Directories" list boxes and then click [Load] to active it.

2. Click [Select Files...] to select files from the backup catalog to be copied back to the hard drive. The "Restore Files" list box indicates which files are being copied. Selecting files to restore is similar to selecting files for a backup.

3. In the "Restore To:" text box, determine where you want to copy back the files you're restoring. Usually this is "Original Locations." However, it's also possible to copy the files to different directories and drives.

4. Click [Options...] to set options for RESTORE.

Before Compressing Your Hard Drive

Chapter Three

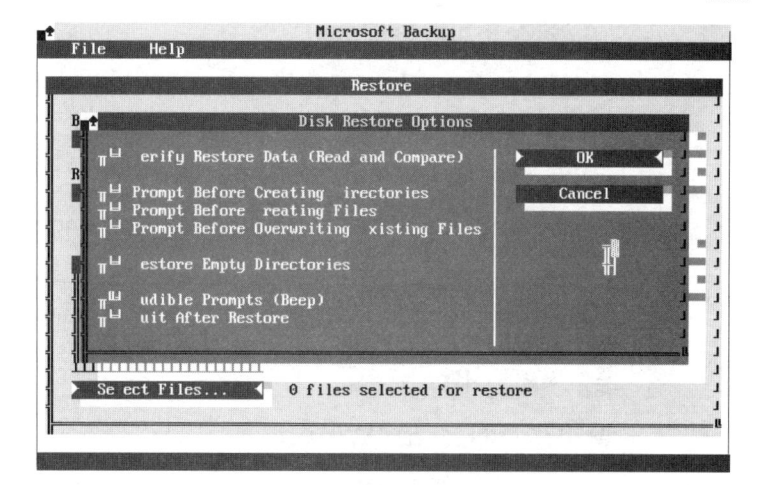

Selecting options

The following settings are possible:

"Verify Restore Data (Read and Compare)"

This setting compares the restored files being copied to the hard drive with the original files on the backup diskettes. This lets you check the results of the restore process.

"Prompt Before Creating Directories"

This setting asks whether you want to create a directory from the backup that is missing on your hard drive.

"Prompt Before Creating Files"

This setting asks whether you want to create backup files that no longer exist on your hard drive.

"Prompt Before Overwriting Existing Files"

This setting asks whether you want the backup files to overwrite versions of the same files on the hard drive.

"Restore Empty Directories"

This setting recreates empty directories from the backup.

Before Compressing Your Hard Drive

Chapter Three

"Audible Prompts (Beep)"

This setting sounds a beep whenever you are supposed to insert a new diskette.

"Quit After Restore"

This setting exits the BACKUP program after the restore is completed.

5. Click the [Start Restore] button to begin restoring your data. The program prompts you to insert diskettes that are identified by the backup number on the label. After all the files are restored, simply exit the BACKUP program.

MSBACKUP for Windows

To make backups with MSBACKUP for Windows, start the program by double-clicking its icon in the Program Manager. The program begins reading the directory tree. Then the Backup start screen appears:

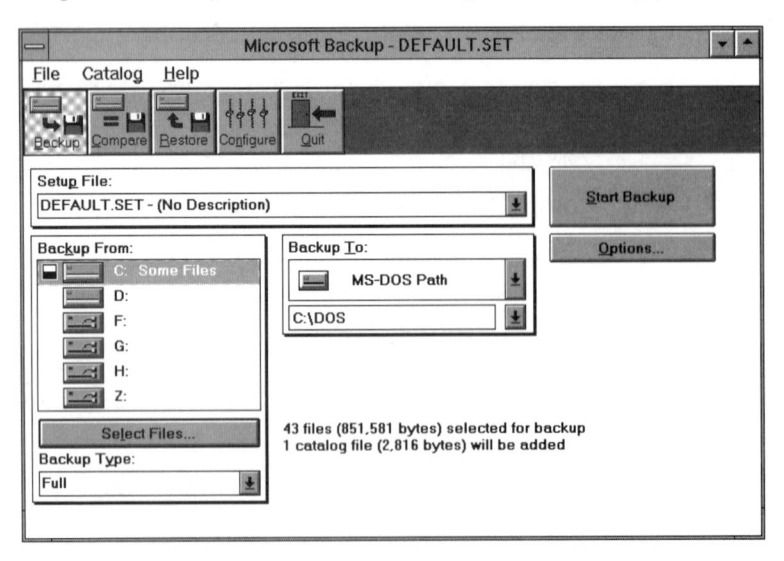

Activating MSBACKUP for Windows

Before Compressing Your Hard Drive

Chapter Three

"Setup File:"

Specifies the configuration file, in which settings such as backup drives and speed are stored. Theoretically, you could be working with several setup files and load a different setup file here.

"Backup To:"

Specifies the disk drive on which you want to create the backups. You should select the drive with the highest capacity.

"Backup From:"

Specifies the hard drive from which you want to make a backup. Usually this is drive C:.

Click [Select Files...], to determine which files will be included in the backup. The "Select Backup Files" dialog box appears.

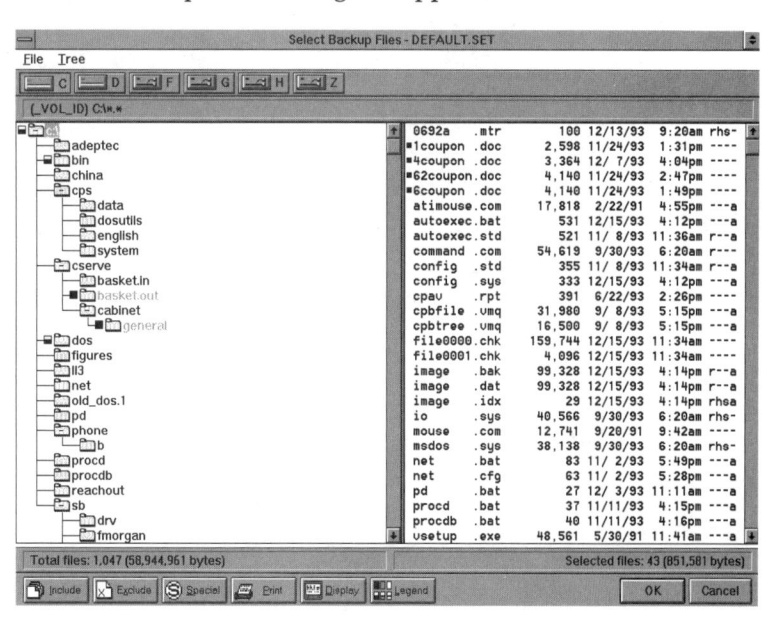

Selecting backup files

There are several ways to select files for the backup:

Before Compressing Your Hard Drive

Chapter Three

1. Manual Selection: In the directory tree, move to the directory that you want to back up. To save all the files in this directory, double-click the directory name.

   In the file list on the right, a checkmark appears in front of the filenames of the selected files. You could also select individual files in the file list.

   To cancel a selection, click the right mouse button. File selection works like a toggle switch. This means that by using exactly the same methods, you can unselect any file that is currently selected.

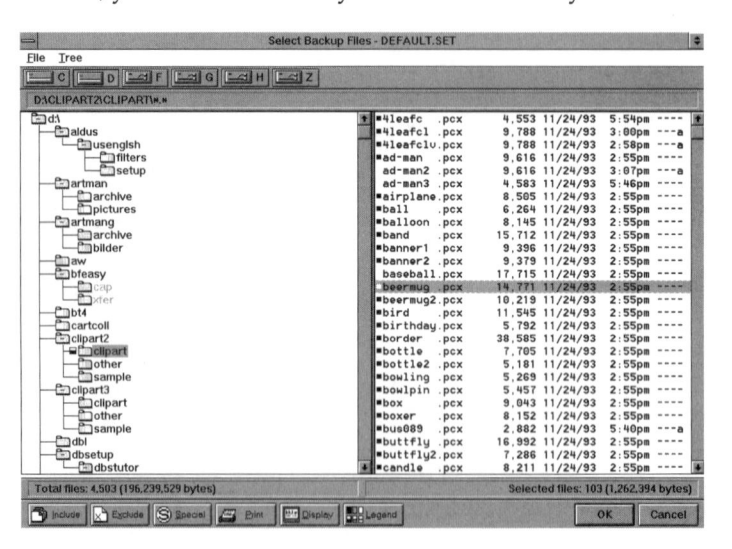

   Selecting files

   Click [Display] to customize the file list.

Before Compressing Your Hard Drive

Chapter Three

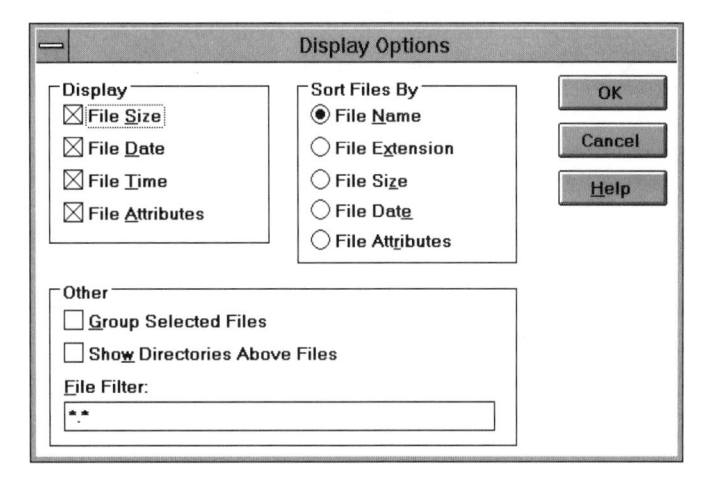

Display options

You can sort files in the list by name, extension, size, date, and attribute. It's also possible to limit files to be displayed by using the "File Filter:" text box. "Group Selected Files" lets you place the selected files of a directory at the beginning of the file list. You can also specify which information is displayed about the files (size, date, time, attributes).

2. Include: Click the [Include] button to determine which files to include in the backup.

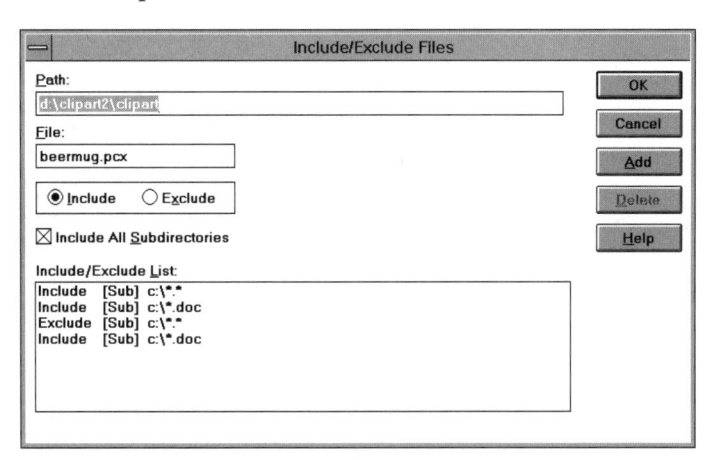

Include dialog box

Before Compressing Your Hard Drive

Chapter Three

Specify the path you want to include in the backup and, if you don't want to back up the complete directory, type a filename after "File:". The "Include All Subdirectories" lets you include the subdirectories of the selected directory in the backup. Click [OK] to confirm the information entered in this dialog box. A checkmark appears in front of the filenames of the selected files.

3. Exclude: Click the [Exclude] button to exclude specific groups of files from a backup.

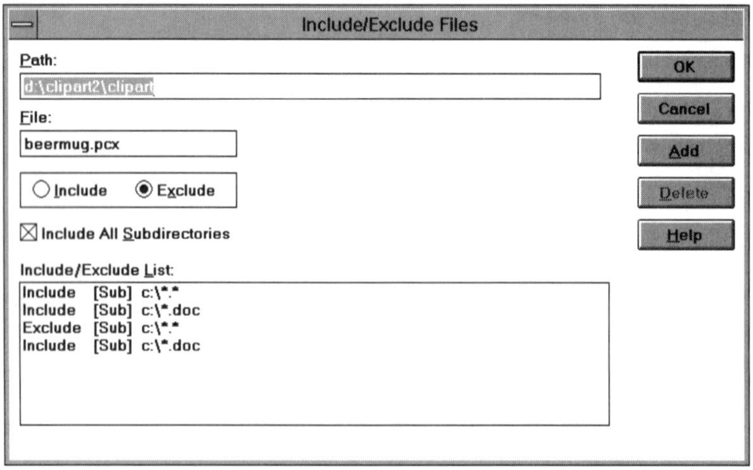

Exclude dialog box

Enter a path and a filename, as you did with "Include" and then confirm by clicking [OK].

4. Special Entries: The [Special] button lets you select files of a specific date range and exclude files with specific attributes.

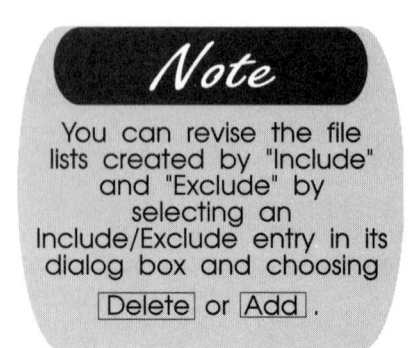

> **Note**
> You can revise the file lists created by "Include" and "Exclude" by selecting an Include/Exclude entry in its dialog box and choosing [Delete] or [Add].

Before Compressing Your Hard Drive

Chapter Three

Special selections

"Backup Files in Date Range"

Lets you back up files between dates specified in the "From:" and "To:" text boxes.

"Exclude Copy Protected Files:"

Excludes the files that you enter in the five text boxes at the lower-right corner of the dialog box. This is a special option for program files that are copy protected.

"Exclude Read-Only Files"

Excludes read-only files from the backup.

"Exclude System Files"

Excludes system files from the backup. For example, it excludes IO.SYS and MSDOS.SYS.

Before Compressing Your Hard Drive

Chapter Three

"Exclude Hidden Files"

Excludes hidden files from the backup. For example, it excludes the IO.SYS and MSDOS.SYS files.

Click [OK] until you return to the Backup screen. After selecting the files for your backup, you can also choose backup options. Click the [Options] button.

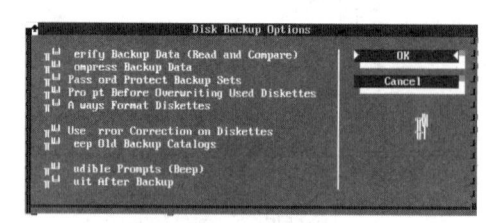

Backup options

The following is an overview of the options:

"Verify Backup Data (Read and Compare)"

Verifies the copied data is correct. If you activate this check box, you don't have to compare the backup data and the original yourself. However, the backup process will take longer.

"Compress Backup Data"

Reduces the amount of disk space required for the backup data on the diskettes. This option reduces the amount of "disk swapping" (taking diskettes in and out of the drive) required during a backup.

"Password Protect Backup Sets"

Protects your backup copies with a password.

"Prompt Before Overwriting Used Diskettes"

Displays a security prompt before overwriting files from an earlier backup.

"Always Format Diskettes"

Automatically formats diskettes during the backup.

Before Compressing Your Hard Drive

Chapter Three

"Use Error Correction on Diskettes"

Increases data security through EEC, a correction procedure that RESTORE is able to use to copy back backup data stored in defective clusters on the diskette.

"Keep Old Backup Catalogs"

Lets you save the old backup catalog (list of all the backup files) on the hard drive.

"Audible Prompts (Beep)"

Causes the computer to beep when it is time for you to insert a new diskette or perform some other activity during the backup.

"Quit After Backup"

Closes the backup program when you're finished performing the backup.

Confirm the settings you've chosen by clicking [OK]. You'll return to the Backup screen. Now you must determine the type of backup.

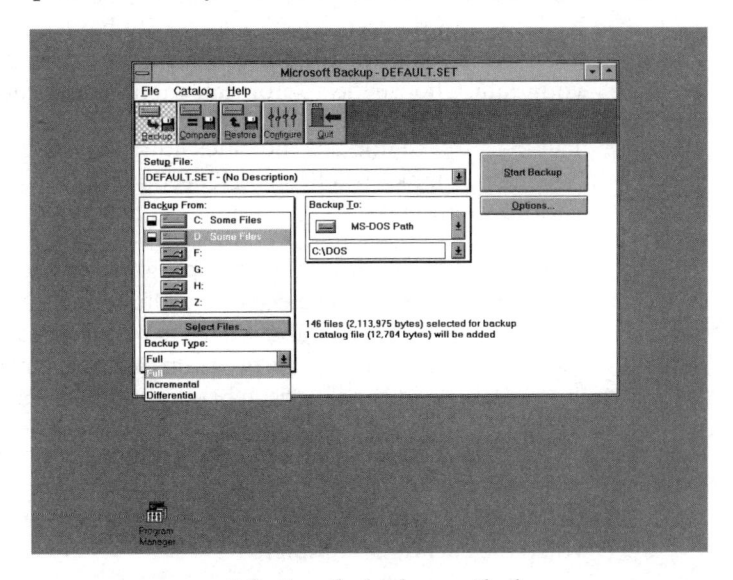

Selecting the backup method

Before Compressing Your Hard Drive

Chapter Three

You can choose from three backup methods:

1. "Full": Backs up all selected files in sequence to a contiguous disk set.

2. "Incremental": Backs up only those selected files that have been changed or added since the last backup. An incremental backup adds to older backups (Full and Incremental) and doesn't overwrite any files. To completely restore your files, you must use the original Full backup and all incremental backups. You can perform any number of incremental backups.

3. "Differential": Also backs up only new files and files that have been changed since the last backup, but a differential backup adds to older backups and also overwrites older versions of backup files.

Your first backup should always be a full backup; otherwise, you'll never have all the necessary data together. You can use the incremental method for your daily backups, but then be sure to perform a full backup once a week.

You could also add to your initial full backup by doing incremental backups, but then you don't necessarily have to perform a full backup every week. Instead, do a full backup once a month, just to keep track of your data. Choose the appropriate method and click [OK].

The "Backup" dialog box indicates how many files are being backed up, how many blank diskettes you'll need for the backup, and how long the backup should take.

Now click [Start Backup]. First, the program creates the backup catalog, based on the files you selected and the type of backup. This catalog is stored on the hard drive and is used to restore files with RESTORE. Now the actual backup starts. The program prompts you to insert diskettes. Be sure to label and number each blank diskette before using it.

During the backup, the program provides information about which diskettes are being accessed, which files are being copied, etc. Simply follow the instructions that appear on the screen and exit the program when the backup is complete.

Before Compressing Your Hard Drive

Chapter Three

Restoring data

Eventually you'll want to copy back the data from the backup to your hard drive. This process is called "restoring." To restore a backup, start the backup program by double-clicking its icon in the Program Manager.

Select "Restore" from the MSBACKUP toolbar. The "Restore" screen appears.

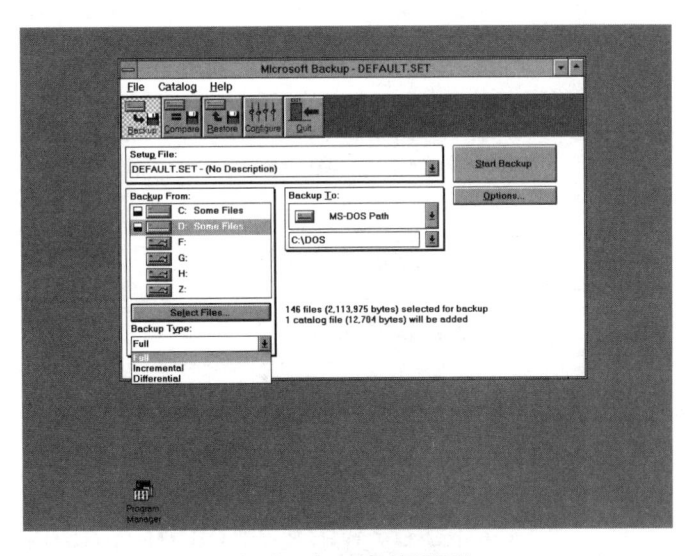

Activating RESTORE

Follow these steps to restore your backup data:

1. Choose a backup catalog, from which you can select the files you want to restore. You should have the catalog files of your last full backup and all subsequent differential and incremental backups as backup sets.

   If you don't (for example, because the catalog files on the hard drive have also been deleted), you must create a catalog file from the backup before doing anything else. To do this, insert the first backup diskette and then open the **Catalog** menu. Then click [Retrieve...] and select the backup drive. The program then reads in the catalog the drive you selected.

Before Compressing Your Hard Drive

Chapter Three

If this won't work (for example, because the first backup diskette is damaged), you can click the (Rebuild...) button. BACKUP then creates a catalog file from the backup. If there is a catalog file on a different drive, you can find and select it in the "Files" and "Directories" list boxes and then click (Load) to activate it.

2. Click (Select Files...) to select files from the backup catalog to be copied back to the hard drive. The "Restore Files" list box shows you which files are being copied. Selecting files to restore is similar to selecting files for a backup.

3. In the "Restore To:" text box, you determine where you want to copy back the files you are restoring. This is usually "Original Locations". However, it's also possible to copy the files to different directories and drives.

4. Click (Options...) to set options for RESTORE.

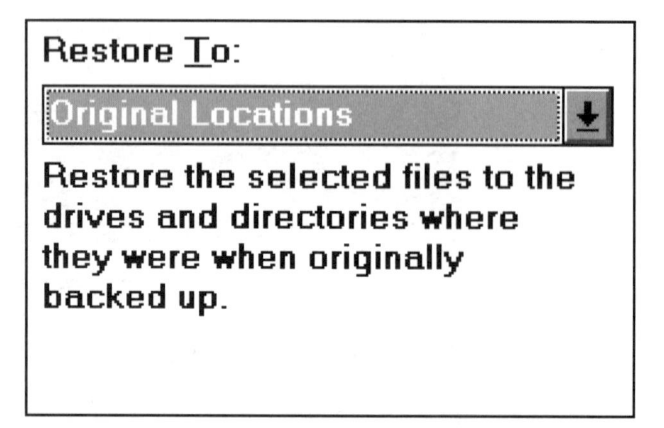

```
Restore To:
┌─────────────────────────────────┐
│ Original Locations            ↓ │
└─────────────────────────────────┘
Restore the selected files to the
drives and directories where
they were when originally
backed up.
```

Options

The following settings are possible:

"Verify Restore Data (Read and Compare)"

Compares the restored files being copied to the hard drive with the original files on the backup diskettes. This lets you check the results of the restore procedure.

Before Compressing Your Hard Drive

Chapter Three

"Prompt Before Creating Directories"

Asks whether you want to create a directory from the backup that is missing on your hard drive.

"Prompt Before Creating Files"

Asks whether you want to create backup files that no longer exist on your hard drive.

"Prompt Before Overwriting Existing Files"

Asks whether you want the backup files to overwrite versions of the same files on the hard drive.

"Restore Empty Directories"

Recreates empty directories from the backup.

"Audible Prompts (Beep)"

Emits a beep whenever you must insert a new diskette.

"Quit After Restore"

Exits the BACKUP program after the restore is completed.

5. Click the [Start Restore] button to begin restoring your data. The program prompts you to insert diskettes that are identified by the backup number on the label. After all the files are restored, simply exit the BACKUP program.

BACKUP and RESTORE

If you're working with DOS 5.0 or an older version, use the BACKUP program to back up your hard drive. To activate this program, select "Backup Fixed Disk" in the DOS Shell or enter the following at the DOS prompt:

BACKUP /PARAMETER [Enter]

Use the drive label of the hard drive you want to back up (usually C:), and the drive letter of the target drive (usually A:) as parameters for BACKUP. The following is the default setting in the DOS Shell:

Before Compressing Your Hard Drive

Chapter Three

```
C: A:
```

If you don't change the parameters and then confirm these changes by pressing [Enter], BACKUP copies all the files in the current directory on the hard drive to the diskette in drive A:. If there are several files in this directory, you may need several diskettes to hold all the data. That's why it's important to remember the following:

- Have enough diskettes available
- Label and number the diskettes

Warning

If a diskette contains important data, don't use it for your backup because this data will be permanently lost.

BACKUP automatically formats the diskettes. This saves you the trouble of formatting them in advance.

You don't have to back up all your files each time you perform a backup. For example, you probably already have backup copies of your programs. In this case, you must back up only your text files. So, when you back up your data, you can find all the text files by adding the following wildcard and extension:

```
C:*.TXT A:
```

You could also use a different extension for Basic programs. You can even back up a single file by typing the filename instead of the wildcard and extension after the source drive:

```
C:EXAMPLE.XMP A:
```

To back up a different directory than the current one, simply include the desired directory:

```
C:\EXAMPLE\*.* a:
```

To back up new files that only match different extensions, after the first backup procedure with file extension A, you must perform additional backup procedures by adding file extensions B, C, etc., to the data of the first backup procedure.

To do this, use the /a switch:

Before Compressing Your Hard Drive

Chapter Three

C:FILENAMEA A: 1. For example, "Texts *.TXT"

C:FILENAMEB A: /A   2. For example, "Program texts *.BAS"

C:FILENAMEC A: /A   3. For example, "Pictures *.PIC"

With the /a switch, all the files will be backed up to a set of diskettes that are numbered sequentially. This occurs even though each backup procedure is handled separately. If you don't use the /a switch, the files will be backed up to three or more sets of diskettes, which always start with "1." This makes it easier to restore the backup data to the hard drive later.

If you perform backups frequently, you can save time by backing up only files that have been changed since the last backup. To do this, enter the following:

```
C:FILENAME A /M /A
```

In this case, BACKUP adds only new data to the existing backup.

If you omit "/A", you'll begin a new set of backup diskettes, starting with "1", in which only modified files are backed up. Then you would have one complete, but old backup and one current, but incomplete backup. That's why you should always use /M with /A to maintain a complete, up-to-date backup.

You can also use the /d and /t time switches to limit the backup even further.

For example, by entering

```
C:FILENAME A: /T:HH:MM:SS /A
```

you can back up all files matching "FILENAME" that have been changed since hh hour, mm minutes, and ss seconds of today and add them to the existing backup.

To back up all files that have changed since MM.DD in the year YY and add them to your backup, enter the following:

```
C:FILENAME A: /D:MM-DD-YY /A
```

Before Compressing Your Hard Drive

Chapter Three

You can use /T and /D together, but you cannot combine them with /M. However, using /M is the easiest method of backing up only new data. Always use /T and /D together with /A.

If you want to include subdirectories in the backup, add the /S switch to the end of the command line:

```
C:FILENAME A: /S
```

You can combine this switch with all the other switches.

The following switch combination can be used the first time a system with a C: hard drive and a disk drive is backed up:

```
C:\FILENAME A: /S
```

We recommend the following combination for future backups:

```
C:\FILENAME A: /S /M /A
```

This ensures that you'll always have a complete backup of your hard drive data on diskette.

After you press (Enter), the backup procedure begins with a prompt to insert a diskette. If this is your first backup, keep inserting diskettes in numerical sequence until DOS no longer prompts you to insert a diskette and the backup is complete.

For all other backups, especially when you use /A, BACKUP prompts you to insert specific diskettes. Be sure to insert the diskette with the correct number. If BACKUP prompts you to insert a diskette with a number that is higher than the number of backup diskettes you have created up to this point, you must prepare a new backup diskette. The amount of data to be backed up has increased.

When you lose data on the hard drive, use the RESTORE program to copy the data from the backup diskette back to the hard drive. In the DOS Shell, select "Restore Fixed Disk" from the DOS Disk Utilities group. Remember that you must use RESTORE after you repartition your hard drive.

Before Compressing Your Hard Drive

Chapter Three

There are also several switches you can use with RESTORE. First, you must specify the source and the target. This time the backup diskette is the source and the hard drive is the target. That's why the DOS Shell has the following switches as the default for RESTORE:

```
A: C:
```

As with BACKUP, you can also use wildcards to specify specific file extensions for the Restore procedure. However, add the wildcard extension to the target drive, not the source drive. For example, type

```
A: C:*.EXE
```

to restore all program files with the .EXE extension to the hard drive. By specifying one specific filename instead of a wildcard, you could also copy back a single file:

```
A: C:EXAMPLE.BSP
```

To include subdirectories in a restore procedure, use the /S switch:

```
A: C:\*.* /S
```

The command line above restores all backup files to the hard drive, including all subdirectories.

To restore all files that were deleted from the hard drive, use the /N switch:

```
A: C: /N
```

The above command restores the hard drive to its previous state, prior to the last file deletions.

Use /M to restore only the files that have been changed since the last backup:

```
A: C: /M
```

Use the following combinations of switches, depending on the situation:

- If you've deleted several files from the hard drive and want to retrieve them from the backup:

Before Compressing Your Hard Drive

Chapter Three

```
A: C:WILDCARD /N /S
```

- If the changes you made to the files are incorrect and you want to restore the original files from the backup:

```
A: C:WILDCARD /M /S
```

- If you've formatted your hard drive and need your data back:

```
A: C:\*.* /S
```

After you choose the right combination of switches and confirm your choice by pressing [Enter], the actual restore process begins. RESTORE prompts you to insert the necessary diskettes. RESTORE uses the numbers on the diskette labels for this purpose. That's why it's very important to label and number your diskettes.

> **Note**
> You cannot use BACKUP and RESTORE with the IO.SYS, MSDOS.SYS, and COMMAND.COM system files. To create backups of these files, you must copy the original DOS diskettes.

MEM and MEMMAKER

Memory allocation is an important aspect of data compression. First you must determine how your computer uses memory. Enter the following command to activate the MEM utility program:

```
MEM [Enter]
```

MEM is included in Version 4.0 and higher of DOS. The program displays a listing of the existing memory types, how much memory is being used, and how much is free.

Before Compressing Your Hard Drive

Chapter Three

MEM memory overview

As little Conventional memory as possible should be used so it's free for DOS programs and applications. However, the Upper memory area should be filled up as much as possible, since it cannot be used for programs and data. As little Extended memory as possible should be occupied, so a lot of memory is free in Windows.

The DOS version you're using and the necessary drivers play a major role in determining what kind of memory allocation is possible on your system. Before Version 5.0 of DOS, it wasn't possible to transfer large components of the operating system to the Upper memory area.

If you don't have Version 6.0 or higher of MS-DOS, you don't have MEMMAKER. Therefore, you can only optimize your computer memory manually.

Try moving more components of DOS to High memory with commands, such as LOADHIGH and DOS=HIGH, in your CONFIG.SYS file. Eliminate drivers that you don't need, such as GRAFTABL. Then restart your computer with your optimized CONFIG.SYS and use MEM to check how the changes affect other settings.

Chapter Three

MEMMAKER

Beginning with DOS 6.0, you can optimize your computer memory automatically with MEMMAKER. However, you must have at least a 386SX processor. MEMMAKER cannot run on older computers.

To run MEMMAKER, do the following:

- Start your computer and all the necessary drivers (for example, the driver software for a network).

- Exit all programs that you don't need, including user interfaces, application programs, and memory resident software.

- At the DOS prompt, enter the following to start MEMMAKER:

MEMMAKER [Enter]

The welcome screen appears.

- Choose [Continue]; the **Setup** menu appears.

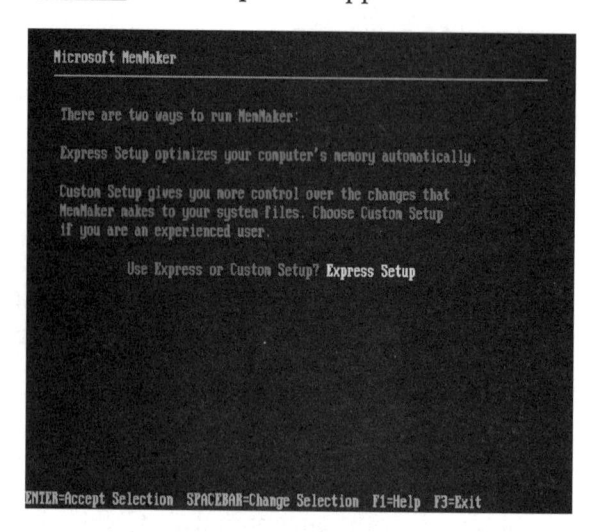

Setup menu

Before Compressing Your Hard Drive

Chapter Three

You can choose between **Express Setup** or **Custom Setup**. Choose **Custom Setup** to have complete access to all the settings. We'll discuss this version of Setup later in the chapter.

- A prompt appears, asking whether you run programs that work with Expanded memory. If you work with Windows, you can answer "No"; most DOS programs don't use Expanded memory. If you aren't sure, choose "No".

- The "Advanced Options" screen appears:

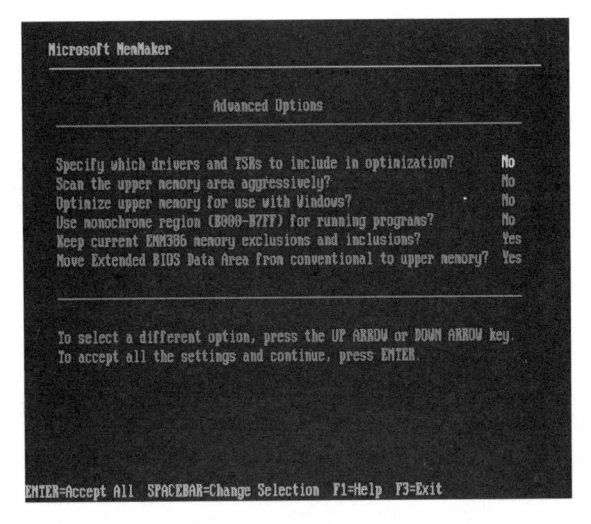

Advanced options

- For each option, you can specify whether you want MEMMAKER to optimize the setting.

Answering the prompts correctly

"Use monochrome region (B000-B7FF) for running programs?"

Answer this prompt with "Yes" if you have an EGA or VGA monitor, but not if you have a SuperVGA monitor.

Before Compressing Your Hard Drive

Chapter Three

"Optimize upper memory for use with Windows"

Answer this prompt with "Yes" only if you never or rarely run DOS programs in Windows.

"Specify which drivers and TSRs to include during optimization"

Answer this prompt with "Yes" only if you crashed during Express setup or if you use a driver that may be incompatible.

- Press [Enter] to continue. MEMMAKER restarts your computer to determine the drivers and DOS components you've been using up to now, along with the memory required by the programs. Press [Enter] and MEMMAKER reboots your computer.

- MEMMAKER starts up again and changes your CONFIG.SYS and AUTOEXEC.BAT files. Then MEMMAKER prompts you to reboot the computer again. This second reboot is necessary to check the changes MEMMAKER made. Press [Enter].

- Now the computer starts up with the new settings. Watch for any error messages that appear. You may have to make some additional changes to the automatic settings manually.

> **Note**
> If the sytem won't start correctly, press the following key combination:
> [Enter] [Alt] [Del]
> This restores the old sytem files and you can restart MEMMAKER.

- MEMMAKER starts up again and asks whether the system is running properly. If there were no errors at startup, answer "Yes" to have MEMMAKER accept the new memory configuration. Otherwise, you can undo the new settings.

- Press [Enter] to exit MEMMAKER.

- Then press [Enter] to confirm MEMMAKER's optimization.

Look at the optimized CONFIG.SYS and AUTOEXEC.BAT files.

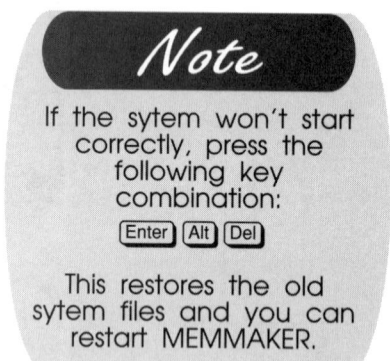

> **Note**
> MEMMAKER also automatically moves the driver for DoubleSpace to High memory.

Before Compressing Your Hard Drive

Chapter Three

AUTOEXEC.BAT optimized with MEMMAKER:

```
@ECHO OFF
PROMPT $p$g
LH /L:0;2,42928 /S C:\DOS\SMARTDRV.EXE
LH /L:2,14064 C:\DOS\SHARE.EXE /F:4096 /L:25
SET PATH=C:\DOS;C:\WINDOWS;C:\WORD;C:\DATA
SET TEMP=C:\WINDOWS\TEMP
SET COMSPEC=C:\DOS\COMMAND.COM
MODE CON CP PREPARE=((850) c:\DOD\EGA.CPI)
MODE CON CP SELECT=850
LH /L:2,16416 KEYB GR,, C:\DOS\KEYBOARD.SYS
LH /L:1,6528 DOSKEY
LH /L:2,56928 MOUSE
CONFIG.SYS optimized with MEMMAKER
DEVICE=C:\DOS\HIMEM.SYS
DEVICE=C:\DOS\EMM386.EXE NOEMS HIGHSCAN I=B000-
B7FF WIN=B500-B7FF WIN=F300-F7FF
BUFFERS=30,0
FILES=40
DOS=UMB
LASTDRIVE=Z
FCBS=16,8
BREAK ON
DOS=HIGH
SHELL=C:\DOS\COMMAND.COM /P /E:1024
STACKS=9,256
DEVICEHIGH=C:\DOS\DISPLAY.SYS CON=(EGA,,1)
DEVICEHIGH=C:\DOS\DBLSPACE.SYS /MOVE
```

Manual changes

You can also gain some memory after running MEMMAKER. Simply optimize the sequence of drivers that are started by CONFIG.SYS and AUTOEXEC.BAT.

Before Compressing Your Hard Drive

Chapter Three

To do this, activate only the drivers that require the most space. If you load MEMMAKER.STS in the DOS directory in a text editor, you can get an overview of what your driver software requires.

Sample MEMMAKER.STS:

```
[MemmakerData]
State= DONE 20301
AvailConvMemoryBefore=590000
AvailUpperMemoryBefore=119392
UsedUpperMemoryBefore=39200
WindowsUpperMemoryBefore=0
EMSUpperMemoryBefore=0
AltSysFiles=False
WindowsXlat=True
CustomMode=True
AutoexecBatCheckSum=31072
ConfigSysCheckSum=30135
SystemIniCheckSum=0
WindowsLocation=c:\windows
 [SizeData]
Command=C:\WINDOWS\WORKGRP.SYS
Line=14
FinalSize=4416
MaxSize=7360
FinalUpperSizes=0
MaxUpperSizes=0
ProgramType=DEVICE
Command=C:\WINDOWS\NE2000.DOS
Line=15
FinalSize=9200
MaxSize=13264
FinalUpperSizes=0
MaxUpperSizes=0
ProgramType=DEVICE
Command=c:\dos\smartdrv.exe
Line=3
```

Before Compressing Your Hard Drive

Chapter Three

```
FinalSize=0
MaxSize=42336
FinalUpperSizes=28816
MaxUpperSizes=42928

ProgramType=PROGRAM
Command=c:\dos\share.exe /f:4096 /l:25
Line=4
FinalSize=7408
MaxSize=14064
FinalUpperSizes=0
MaxUpperSizes=0
ProgramType=PROGRAM
Command=keyb gr,, c:\dos\keyboard.sys
Line=10
FinalSize=6224
MaxSize=16416
FinalUpperSizes=0
MaxUpperSizes=0
ProgramType=PROGRAM
Command=doskey
Line=11
FinalSize=4160
MaxSize=6528
FinalUpperSizes=0
MaxUpperSizes=0
ProgramType=PROGRAM
Command=mouse
Line=12
FinalSize=17088
MaxSize=56928
FinalUpperSizes=0
MaxUpperSizes=0
ProgramType=PROGRAM
```

Before Compressing Your Hard Drive

Chapter Three

The maximum amount of memory required by the driver is listed after "MaxSize." Shift the drivers in the configuration files around according to size. This provides a better system configuration.

> **Note**
>
> You can shift all the drives.
>
> You can move network drivers, but only as a group.

HIMEM.SYS and EMM386.EXE must come before all other drivers and programs. SETVER.EXE can only follow HIMEM.SYS and EMM386.EXE if you aren't using any other memory manager besides these two. If SETVER.EXE follows these two drivers, the program can be executed in High memory.

Although you can move network drivers, it must be as a group. For example, if three drivers are needed to make the network active, as is the case with Windows for Workgroups, then these drivers must remain in their original order, one after the other. However, you can shift the group.

ScanDisk (DOS 6.2 and above)

ScanDisk checks your hard drive for errors and repairs them. It locates destroyed sectors, lost clusters, and other types of damage and removes them from your hard drive. DoubleSpace automatically runs ScanDisk, but you can also run ScanDisk yourself. To do this, type the following from the DOS prompt (never run ScanDisk except from the DOS prompt):

SCANDISK [Enter]

Now the program checks the following five items:

- Volume
- File Allocation Tables (FATs)
- File System
- Directory Structure
- Surface Structure

Before Compressing Your Hard Drive

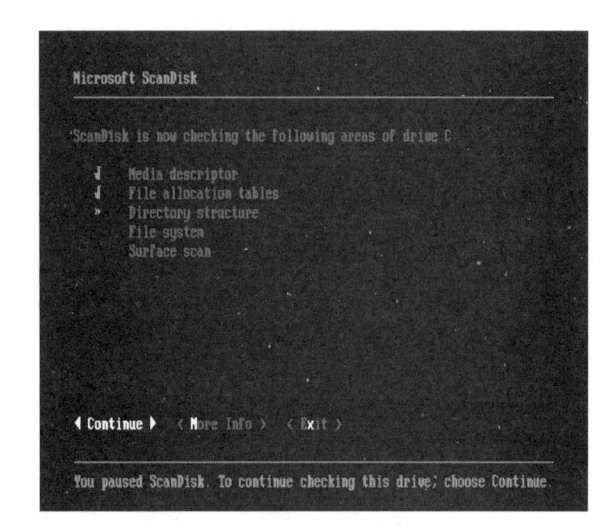

Chapter Three

ScanDisk Screen

When ScanDisk is finished, you can also run a surface scan. The program reads and writes each sector of the hard drive, similar to DEFRAG.

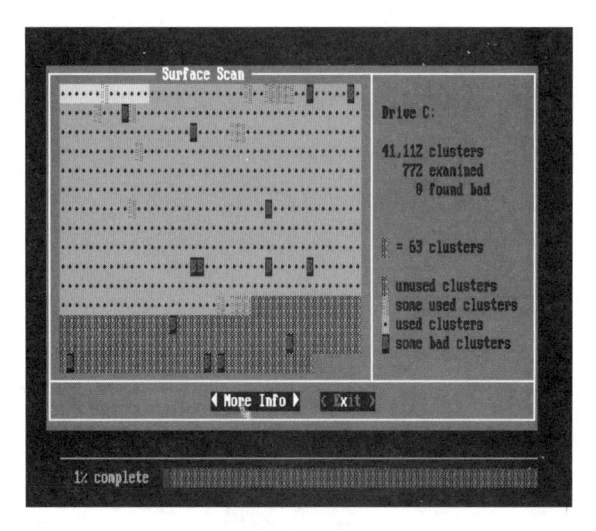

ScanDisk Surface Scan

Then ScanDisk automatically closes.

Chapter 4

DoubleSpace

Contents

Installing DoubleSpace 83

Using Compressed Drives 97

Managing Compressed Drives 101

Optimizing Your Hard Drive 116

DOS 6.2 Additions 122

DoubleSpace and Other Applications 123

Common Error Messages 128

Removing DoubleSpace 131

Uncompressing Drives (DOS 6.2) 132

DoubleSpace

Chapter Four

So far you've read about the fundamentals and techniques of data compression and have learned about the DOS utility programs that provide valuable data compression functions.

In this chapter, we'll discuss compression itself and focus on DoubleSpace. We'll explain how to install DoubleSpace and how to use it to manage compressed drives. DoubleSpace is included with all versions of DOS 6, including updates, upgrades, and full versions.

Installing DoubleSpace

Installing a compressed drive with DoubleSpace is more complicated than installing standard software. After all, direct online compression of a drive represents quite a disruption of your system and requires the proper preparation.

> **Note**
> Before installing DoubleSpace, read Chapter 3. Also, you should be very familiar with the FDISK, FORMAT, CHKDSK, BACKUP, RESTORE and MEMMAKER programs. Otherwise, you won't be able to install DoubleSpace successfully.

Start your computer and exit all interfaces, such as the DOS Shell or Windows, until you are at the DOS prompt. You can only install DoubleSpace and prepare your hard drive safely and quickly at the DOS prompt.

Checking partitions

First, check the number and type of existing partitions. Since you're going to install at least one more drive with DoubleSpace, you must delete any additional logical drives created by DOS partitions. Otherwise, you'll have too many drive labels. To check the partitions, start the FDISK utility program.

Chapter Four

Checking the partitions

If you have only a primary DOS partition, everything is fine. You can exit FDISK and move on to the next step.

Use FDISK to delete any other unnecessary partitions. If you also work with IBM's OS/2 operating system, you need an OS/2 partition. If you're using SpeedStor, this program will also require a special partition. Besides these two exceptions, you should delete any partitions that you don't need.

However, when you delete partitions, you have a problem because you cannot simply add the resulting free disk space to the first primary DOS partition. It's not possible to change the partition sizes afterwards. Therefore, you must first delete all the partitions and then create a single new partition.

Since deleting a partition also means losing the data that was on the partition, you must perform a complete backup of your hard drive before deleting the partitions. Otherwise, you'll lose all your data when you repartition your hard drive.

After you finish repartitioning your hard drive, reformat the hard drive and copy the data back to the hard drive. Then you're ready for the next step.

DoubleSpace

Chapter Four

Deleting unnecessary files

Creating a compressed drive shouldn't be like moving to a larger house. You don't have to hoard everything, even if you do have a lot of space. Therefore, don't hesitate to delete any files and programs that you never use. If you don't think you have anything that fits this description on your system, take a good look at your hard drive.

Remember that files with the following extensions are unnecessary and must be deleted before you compress your hard drive:

TMP	Temporary files
CHK	Files created by CHKDSK or SCANDSK
BAK	Program backup files
OLD	Older versions of files

DOS and Windows also come with many useless files.

Sample BASIC programs

For example, have you ever worked with QBasic and taken a look at the sample programs, such as GORILLA.BAS? If you haven't used these programs, then delete all the .BAS BASIC files in your DOS directory.

BMP wallpaper files

Do you use all the BMP wallpaper files in Windows? If not, delete the ones you don't need.

DOS Shell

If you never use the DOS Shell and prefer PC Tools, Norton Commander, or Windows, then delete the DOS Shell. The following command removes all partial programs of the Shell:

```
ERASE DOSSHELL.* Enter
```

Chapter Four

Laptop files

If you're not running DOS on a laptop, then you don't need POWER.EXE, INTERLNK.*, and INTERSVR.* either. Delete these files.

DOS utility programs

Several DOS utility programs may also be unnecessary. For example, have you ever used ATTRIB, CHCP, CTTY, DEBUG, DISKCOMP, EDIT (DOS text editor), EXPAND, FASTOPEN, FC, GRAPHICS, MSCDEX, MSD, NLSFUNC, PRINT, QBASIC, SORT, SYS, or VERIFY? If you rarely use these programs, simply move them to a backup diskette and them delete them from your hard drive.

Extensive help systems

Many application programs include extensive help systems. If you're already thoroughly familiar with an application, you probably don't use its help feature very often. In this case, delete the help files you don't need. You'll save a few megabytes (almost 2 Meg for Excel help, 1 Meg for WinWord help, 4 Meg for Access help).

Sample database files

Today, sample databases are also quite large. If you removed, for example, all the sample files of FoxPro for Windows, you would reduce the disk space required for FoxPro by half.

Dictionaries and thesauruses

Finally, many dictionaries and thesauruses are extremely large. Although these are important tools for word processing, you may not use them regularly. If you can do without your thesauruses and dictionaries, delete the directory files with the .THS and .LEX extensions.

This also applies to grammar checkers. If you eliminate these files, you'll gain a couple megabytes of free disk space. However, you will need to weigh the consequences of this action. Is the free storage space worth the loss of these valuable tools?

DoubleSpace

Chapter Four

Since it's only possible to create compressed drives when the hard drive has at least some free memory, you need to take this step (cleaning out your hard drive) of the process seriously.

Also, creating a compressed drive on a hard drive with allocated memory is time-consuming. Therefore, it's better to compress memory that is already free. Get as much free disk space on your hard drive as you possibly can. The more free disk space, the larger your new compressed drive can be.

Removing CHK files

The second step is only applicable to systems running versions earlier than DOS 6 and requires removing all the lost clusters from the hard drive you're compressing. Systems running DOS 6 may use SCANDISK for this purpose.

To do this, activate the DOS CHKDSK utility program with the /F switch. Then use **Delete** to remove the .CHK files.

CHKDSK is used not only for compression, but also for defragmenting the hard drive.

Defragmenting

Now you're ready to defragment the hard drive. With DOS 5.0 and earlier versions, you must use one of the utility programs from PC Tools (COMPRESS) or Norton Utilities (DEFRAG). DOS 6 includes its own defragmenting program called DEFRAG.

Activate DEFRAG and select the recommended optimization.

DoubleSpace

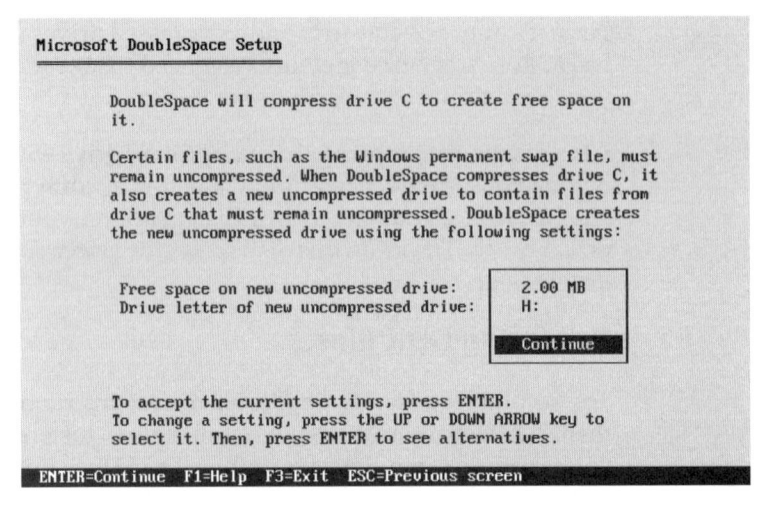

Chapter Four

Defragmenting the hard drive

Installing a compressed drive works much better on an optimized hard drive than it does on a hard drive that hasn't been optimized. After running CHKDSK and DEFRAG, reboot your computer.

Starting the installation

DoubleSpace provides several kinds of installation. So before you begin, you must determine which type of installation is best for your system.

Important considerations

When you compress your hard drive, you want to gain as much disk space as possible in the shortest amount of time.

Some file types, such as database, text, and graphic files, compress better than other file types. These file types contain much information that is redundant, so it's easy to reduce their size. However, you don't waste much time compressing and decompressing, because, except for databases, such files are usually relatively small. Therefore, write and read operations are fast.

With databases, the entire file isn't usually affected by read or write operations. Instead, only a group of data records is affected, so compression doesn't take long with databases either.

DoubleSpace

Chapter Four

However, generally the contents of a hard drive don't consist of just databases, texts, and graphics. The data mainly consists of programs. For example, while this book takes up only about half a Meg of disk space, the word processor we used to create and format the book requires almost six megabytes.

Programs can't be compressed very much, and the time spent compressing them needlessly slows down the execution of the applications. Therefore, you shouldn't compress program files at all.

Besides, there are some program and system files that you can't compress if you want to keep your system running. Among these files are COMMAND.COM, IO.SYS, and MSDOS.SYS, as well as the permanent Windows swap file. Therefore, you'll never be able to compress the entire hard drive. At least 1.7 Meg must be kept free on your startup drive.

Also, you should always keep some free, uncompressed memory available on your hard drive for emergencies. For example, you may want to install a program that can't work with a compressed hard drive. Or perhaps you have documents or databases that are so large, they take too much time to compress.

Now, let's review what we've learned: 1) Compress only document files. 2) Never compress your entire hard drive. As a result, we don't recommend using Express Setup when you install DoubleSpace. Express Setup attempts to compress as much of your hard drive as possible.

Custom Setup provides two choices: You can either compress an existing drive or create a new empty compressed drive.

When you choose the first option, DoubleSpace compresses the C: hard drive, including all of its files. The last two megabytes of the hard drive aren't compressed and are configured as drive D:. All the files that cannot be compressed are copied to this new D: drive. The compressed volume file (CVF) becomes part of drive D:. Drive D: becomes the new startup drive.

With the second option, DoubleSpace first creates a new D: drive with the free disk space on drive C:. Then DoubleSpace compresses drive D:. Other than that, nothing else changes.

DoubleSpace

Chapter Four

We recommend using the second option for two reasons: 1) You don't have to make any adjustments in using the program and the system. After all, drive C: is still drive C: and all your programs and system files remain on this drive; 2) You decide which files will be moved to the compressed drive. This way, you can compress only those files that can be compressed tightly.

The disadvantage of this option is that DoubleSpace can use only the free disk space on the hard drive to create a new, compressed drive. So you need to free up as much memory as possible before using DoubleSpace (refer to the section called "Deleting unnecessary files").

However, there's another alternative: First create the compressed drive at the maximum size. Then move files from drive C:, which is uncompressed, to the compressed drive, D:. This saves you disk space, because usually compressed files on D: take up only half the memory of drive C:. So drive C: has free memory again.

Then you can use DoubleSpace to add the free memory on C: to the compressed drive. (For more information, refer to the section on using compressed drives in MS-DOS). By doing this, you can compensate for the disadvantage of using the second option.

Now let's install DoubleSpace according to the method we discussed.

1. Activate DoubleSpace at the DOS prompt by entering:

```
DBLSPACE
```

If this is the first time you've called DoubleSpace, the Setup screen appears; otherwise the DoubleSpace management screen is displayed. If this occurs, select **Create New Drive** from the **Compress** menu. Then continue with Step 4.

2. Press [Enter]. A menu appears, in which you can choose either Custom or Express Setup. Choose **Custom Setup**.

3. Another menu appears, in which you can choose between **Compress an Existing drive** and **Create a new empty compressed drive**. Select **Create a new empty compressed drive**.

DoubleSpace

Chapter Four

4. A list of the existing drives appears. Choose the drive (host drive) that will provide the disk space for the compressed volume file.

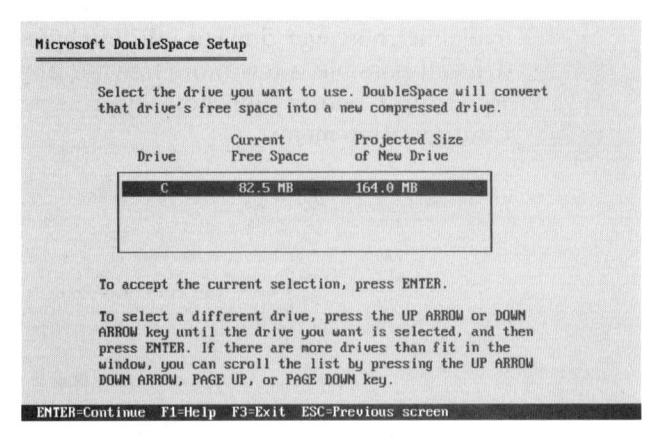

```
Microsoft DoubleSpace Setup

    Select the drive you want to use. DoubleSpace will convert
    that drive's free space into a new compressed drive.

                   Current          Projected Size
        Drive      Free Space       of New Drive

          C         82.5 MB          164.0 MB



    To accept the current selection, press ENTER.

    To select a different drive, press the UP ARROW or DOWN
    ARROW key until the drive you want is selected, and then
    press ENTER. If there are more drives than fit in the
    window, you can scroll the list by pressing the UP ARROW
    DOWN ARROW, PAGE UP, or PAGE DOWN key.

 ENTER=Continue  F1=Help  F3=Exit  ESC=Previous screen
```

Selecting a drive

5. The **Configuration** menu appears. In this menu, you can choose how much free memory will be left on the host drive after creating the compressed drive. You set the expected compression ratio to an estimate of the amount of disk space gained by compression and choose the drive letter for the compressed drive you're creating.

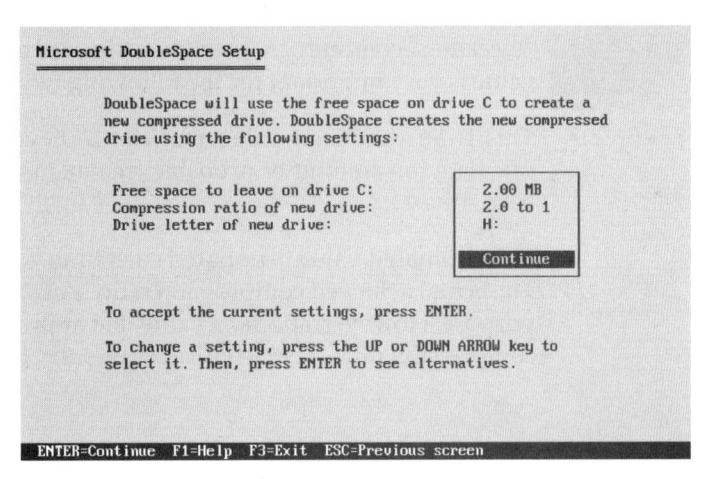

```
Microsoft DoubleSpace Setup

    DoubleSpace will use the free space on drive C to create a
    new compressed drive. DoubleSpace creates the new compressed
    drive using the following settings:

    Free space to leave on drive C:         2.00 MB
    Compression ratio of new drive:         2.0 to 1
    Drive letter of new drive:              H:
                                          Continue

    To accept the current settings, press ENTER.

    To change a setting, press the UP or DOWN ARROW key to
    select it. Then, press ENTER to see alternatives.

 ENTER=Continue  F1=Help  F3=Exit  ESC=Previous screen
```

Configuration menu

Chapter Four

6. Select the first setting to determine the amount of remaining free memory on the host drive. The default setting of 2 Meg is the minimum for a startup drive; otherwise 1 Meg is sufficient. As we explained, however, don't use all your bytes for the compressed hard drive. If possible, a few more free megabytes of memory certainly won't hurt. Confirm your choice by pressing [Enter]. You'll return to the **Configuration** menu.

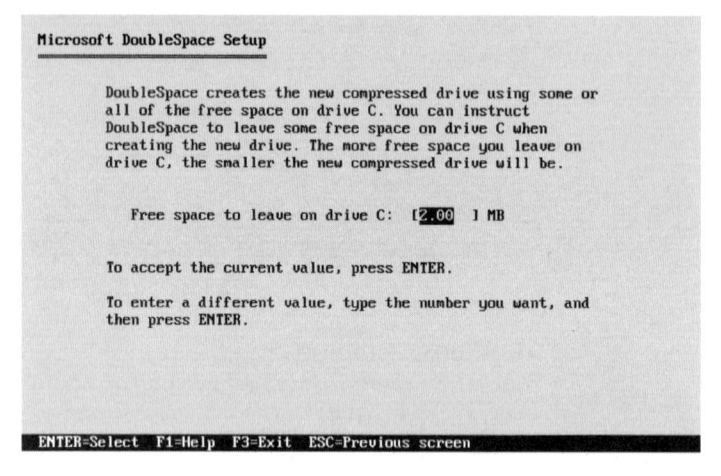

```
Microsoft DoubleSpace Setup

         DoubleSpace creates the new compressed drive using some or
         all of the free space on drive C. You can instruct
         DoubleSpace to leave some free space on drive C when
         creating the new drive. The more free space you leave on
         drive C, the smaller the new compressed drive will be.

         Free space to leave on drive C:  [2.00  ] MB

         To accept the current value, press ENTER.

         To enter a different value, type the number you want, and
         then press ENTER.



 ENTER=Select  F1=Help  F3=Exit  ESC=Previous screen
```

Defining the free space

7. Select the second entry to enter the estimated compression ratio. This value is very important for the following two reasons:

- This is an estimated value that the DOS command DIR uses to calculate the amount of probable free memory on the compressed hard drive.

- This estimated value is updated each time you start up the system. The actual achieved compression ratio is used as a reference for this purpose. However, specify a value that approximates the estimated compression ratio. Then confirm your entry by pressing [Enter].

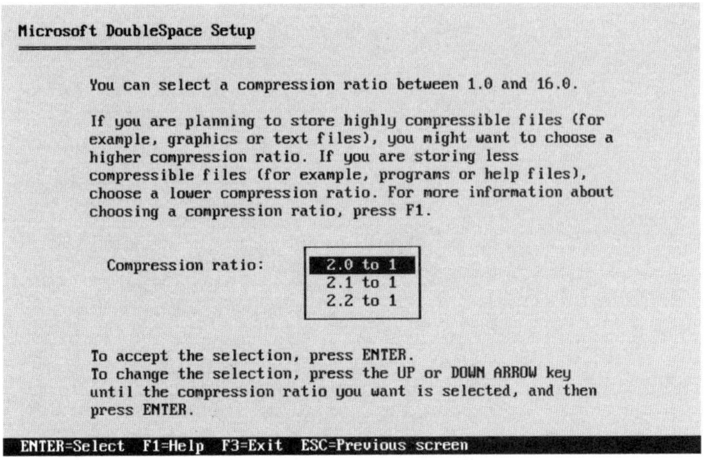

DoubleSpace

Chapter Four

```
Microsoft DoubleSpace Setup

    You can select a compression ratio between 1.0 and 16.0.

    If you are planning to store highly compressible files (for
    example, graphics or text files), you might want to choose a
    higher compression ratio. If you are storing less
    compressible files (for example, programs or help files),
    choose a lower compression ratio. For more information about
    choosing a compression ratio, press F1.

              Compression ratio:    ┌─────────┐
                                    │ 2.0 to 1│
                                    │ 2.1 to 1│
                                    │ 2.2 to 1│
                                    └─────────┘

    To accept the selection, press ENTER.
    To change the selection, press the UP or DOWN ARROW key
    until the compression ratio you want is selected, and then
    press ENTER.

 ENTER=Select  F1=Help  F3=Exit  ESC=Previous screen
```

Setting the compression ratio

8. Finally, choose the last entry in the **Configuration** menu to assign a drive letter to your new compressed drive. Be sure to choose a letter that isn't already being used. Remember, logical drives, such as network drives and RAM drives, already have letters.

   Also, be sure your letter doesn't come after the letter specified in the Lastdrive entry of the CONFIG.SYS file. For example, if your entry reads "Lastdrive=E", then your compressed drive should be either D or E.

   If you don't have any drives free, cancel the installation, increase the value for Lastdrive, and start the installation again. Once you've chosen a drive letter for your compressed drive, confirm your selection with [Enter]; you'll return to the **Configuration** menu.

Chapter Four

```
Microsoft DoubleSpace Setup

    DoubleSpace is ready to create drive H, a new compressed
    drive, using the free space on drive C. This will take about
    14 minutes.

    During this process, DoubleSpace will restart your computer
    to load DBLSPACE.BIN, the portion of MS-DOS that provides
    access to DoubleSpace compressed drives.


    To create the new compressed drive, press C.
    To return to the previous screen, press ESC.




 C=Continue  F1=Help  F3=Exit  ESC=Previous screen
```

DoubleSpace is ready to create the new drive

9. Now select the **Continue** command in the **Configuration** menu.

10. A security prompt appears. Among other information, you'll learn how long it will take to create the compressed drive. This estimate of the time needed is valid only if you ran CHKDSK and DEFRAG before DoubleSpace. Press [C] for "Continue".

11. DoubleSpace automatically runs CHKDSK. (If you didn't run CHKDSK beforehand and file clusters appear, DoubleSpace will stop running.) Next, the program automatically runs DEFRAG. (If you already ran DEFRAG, this process won't take too long.) DoubleSpace then restarts the computer and creates a compressed drive. The changes in the CONFIG.SYS and AUTOEXEC.BAT files become effective when the computer restarts.

Note
If your computer doesn't reboot, press [Ctrl] [Alt] [Del]

DoubleSpace

Chapter Four

Now you have a new, empty compressed drive on your system. DoubleSpace created a hidden file called "DBLSPACE.00?." This hidden file contains your compressed drive. A file in Conventional memory, called "DBLSPACE.BIN", makes it possible for you to control your compressed drive. You'll find the following line in your CONFIG.SYS file:

```
DEVICE=C:\DOS\DBLSPACE.SYS
```

This line places "DBLSPACE.BIN" in Conventional memory as a memory resident program.

In the next section, we'll explain how to use your new drive. However, first you must optimize your memory.

Optimizing memory

The standard installation of DoubleSpace sends the DBLSPACE.BIN file to Conventional memory (up to 640K). If you use large DOS programs, this solution isn't the best because a lot of memory cannot be used by DoubleSpace. If you have more than 640K of RAM, you can move DoubleSpace to High memory. To do this, change the line in your CONFIG.SYS to the following:

```
DEVICEHIGH=C:\DOS\DBLSPACE.SYS /MOVE
```

It's also possible to make this and other optimizations automatically. To do this, call the MEMMAKER utility program by entering the following:

```
MEMMAKER Enter
```

The program places DBLSPACE.BIN in High memory and rearranges the rest of your system memory.

For more information about MEMMAKER, refer to Chapter 3.

Converting compressed drives to DoubleSpace format

Obviously, DoubleSpace isn't the first software program for compressing data. However, DoubleSpace is the first compression software that is an integral part of the operating system. Perhaps you've already been using a different data compression program, such as DoubleDensity, Stacker,

Chapter Four

XtraDrive, with an older version of DOS. If you've updated to DOS 6.2, you may want to convert your compressed drive to DoubleSpace format. To do this, follow these steps:

1. Install MS-DOS 6.2.

2. Use the MSBACKUP command to back up the files on your hard drive.

3. Insert Setup diskette 1 in drive A: and then reboot your computer by pressing Ctrl + Alt + Del. When the first screen appears, press 3 twice to exit Setup.

4. Use the FORMAT command to format the drive containing the file used to store all your compressed files. If you reformat drive C:, specify the /S switch to transfer your system files.

5. After formatting drive C:, insert Setup diskette 1 in drive A: or B: and enter the following at the system prompt:

    A:SETUP Enter

    or

    B:SETUP Enter

    Then follow the instructions that appear on the screen.

    > **Note**
    > If your computer is using XtraDrive device driver compression, run the appropriate uninstall program to remove the compression. Then install DoubleSpace.

6. After Setup is complete, install DoubleSpace by entering the following at the system prompt:

    DBLSPACE Enter

    Follow the instructions on the screen.

7. Now restore the files you backed up earlier.

DoubleSpace

Chapter Four

Using Compressed Drives

Using a compressed drive is easier than you might think. DoubleSpace ensures that the compressed drive acts like an ordinary drive on file managers, such as the DOS Shell, PC Tools, or Norton Commander, on user interfaces, such as Windows and Geoworks Ensemble, as well as on application programs and DOS itself.

For example, if you want to save a file from your word processor to the compressed drive, the compressed drive appears as a normal drive entry in the "Drives:" list box of the "Save As" dialog box. For example, it will appear as D: or E:. The conventional filenames and extensions apply here.

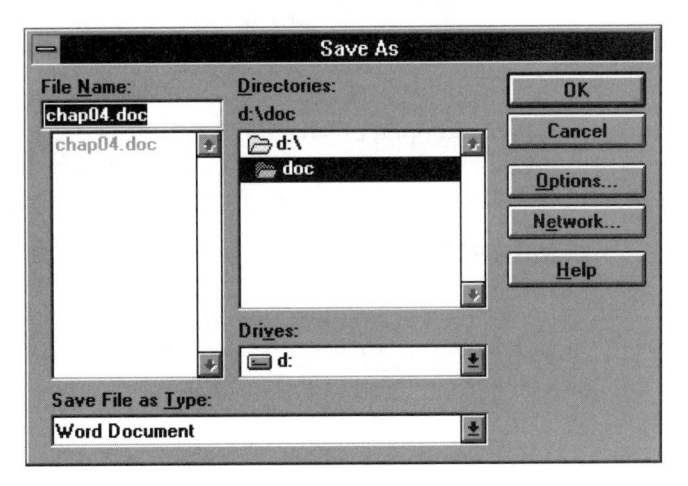

Saving a file to a compressed drive

Opening compressed files is as easy. They appear as normal files in the "File Name:" list box of the "Open" dialog box:

DoubleSpace

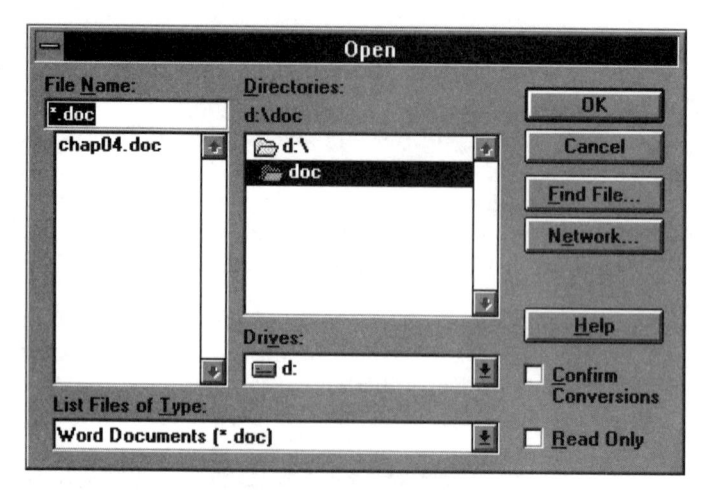

Chapter Four

Opening a compressed file

When you open or save a file, DoubleSpace works in the background, invisibly decompressing or compressing the data. This applies for both DOS programs and Windows applications.

MS-DOS

In DOS, you can address DoubleSpace drives just like normal hard drives and diskettes. For example, if your compressed drive is D:, then you can change to this drive by entering:

```
D: Enter
```

Enter the following command to display the contents of the drive:

```
DIR Enter
```

Aside from the fact that compressed drives are named "Compressed" by default, nothing indicates that the data is compressed. You can even change the name of the drive using the DOS LABEL command.

To move files from uncompressed drives to your compressed drive, enter:

```
MOVE C:DATA D: Enter
```

DoubleSpace

Chapter Four

To set up a directory on your compressed hard drive, use the MD command:

`MD DIRECTORY` [Enter]

To change directories on your compressed hard drive, use the CD command:

`CD DIRECTORY` [Enter]

If you saved files on the compressed hard drive, a special option of DIR will help you determine the degree of compression. Enter the following

`DIR /C` [Enter]

to have DOS display the degree of compression for each file and the average compression ratio.

> **Note**
> Remember to replace "DATA" with the actual filename(s) of the data you want moved.

> **Note**
> Do not delete or rename any files beginning with "DBLSPACE." These are system, initialization, and configuration files of DoubleSpace and of the compressed hard drive. To prevent data loss, handle these files carefully.

```
CHAP3_27 TIF       291,377 12-15-93   4:43p   12.5 to 1.0
CHAP3_28 TIF       161,587 12-15-93   4:43p   10.0 to 1.0
CHAP3_29 TIF         9,417 12-15-93   4:44p   10.7 to 1.0
CHAP3_30 TIF       788,787 12-15-93   4:46p   12.8 to 1.0
CHAP3_32 TIF        41,271 12-16-93  11:32a    8.7 to 1.0
CHAP3_31 TIF       262,055 12-16-93  11:43a   10.9 to 1.0
CHAP3_33 TIF       338,022 12-16-93  12:06p   10.0 to 1.0
CHAP3_34 TIF       338,022 12-16-93  12:20p    9.7 to 1.0
CHAP3_37 TIF       338,022 12-16-93   1:12p    9.5 to 1.0
CHAP3_36 TIF       338,022 12-16-93   1:03p   11.0 to 1.0
CHAP3_35 TIF       338,022 12-16-93   1:27p    8.0 to 1.0
CHAP4_01 TIF       128,302 12-16-93   3:12p    8.5 to 1.0
CHAP4_02 TIF       128,302 12-16-93   3:13p    7.8 to 1.0
CHAP4_03 TIF       128,302 12-16-93   3:13p    8.3 to 1.0
CHAP4_04 TIF       128,302 12-16-93   3:14p    8.5 to 1.0
CHAP4_05 TIF       128,302 12-16-93   3:14p    8.5 to 1.0
CHAP4_06 TIF       128,302 12-16-93   3:15p    8.0 to 1.0
CHAP4_07 TIF       128,302 12-16-93   3:15p    9.1 to 1.0
CHAP4_08 TIF        59,638 12-16-93   3:43p    8.5 to 1.0
CHAP4_09 TIF        59,495 12-16-93   3:42p    8.5 to 1.0
                  8.7 to 1.0 average compression ratio
       48 file(s)       9,019,736 bytes
                      241,459,200 bytes free

D:\FIGS>
```

Calling DIR /C

DoubleSpace

Chapter Four

You must use DoubleSpace for any additional management of your compressed drive. For more information, refer to the "Managing Compressed Drives" section in this chapter.

MS-Windows

It's even easy to manage compressed drives in Windows. Activate the File Manager by double-clicking the appropriate icon in the Program Manager. In the drive icon bar, you'll immediately see the compressed drive highlighted as a new hard drive.

Choose the **Create Directory...** command in the **File** menu to create new directories. Double-click the directory icons to change between directories of the compressed drive.

Use the **Copy** and **Move** commands in the **File** menu to place files on the compressed hard drive and remove them. The same commands, such as Delete and Rename, that are available for an uncompressed drive are also available for your compressed drive. Also, information about the files will be correct.

The File Manager contains a new menu called "Tools." In this menu, you will find the **DoubleSpace Info...** command, which displays the following dialog box when you select it:

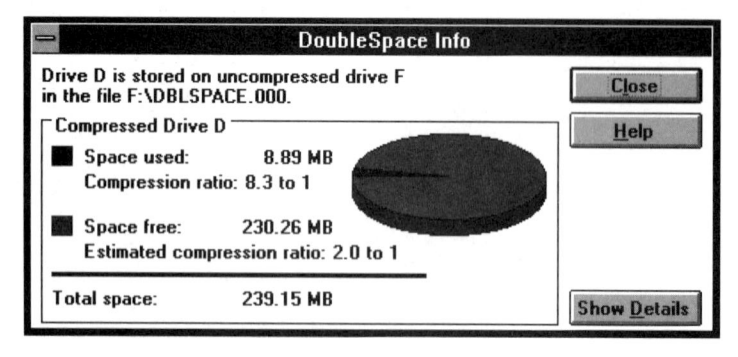

DoubleSpace Info dialog box

DoubleSpace

Chapter Four

This dialog box illustrates the relationship between the used memory on your compressed drive and the total free memory on your hard drive. The name of the file containing the compressed drive appears at the top of the dialog box.

Choose one of the following buttons to get information about the dialog box:

- Used Memory
- Free Memory
- Total Memory
- Show Details

Press 1 for more information about these buttons.

Warning: Do not delete or rename any files beginning with "DBLSPACE." These are system, initialization, and configuration files of DoubleSpace and of the compressed hard drive. To prevent data loss, handle these files carefully.

Use DoubleSpace for any additional management of your compressed drive. For more information, see the "Managing Compressed Drives" section in this chapter.

Managing Compressed Drives

The DoubleSpace program is responsible for managing compressed drives. This involves defragmenting, verifying, enlarging, and reducing drives as well as deleting them. Remember that this isn't the same DoubleSpace program you learned about when you installed your first compressed drive. That was the DoubleSpace Setup program.

Note: You can also call DoubleSpace commands from the DOS prompt. The parameters for DoubleSpace commands are listed in Chapter 6.

Never use DoubleSpace from Windows, the DOS Shell, or any other DOS interface. Always activate DoubleSpace from the DOS prompt. DoubleSpace has a menu-driven interface, which we'll describe in this chapter.

Chapter Four

Start DoubleSpace by entering:

DBLSPACE [Enter]

The DoubleSpace welcome screen appears:

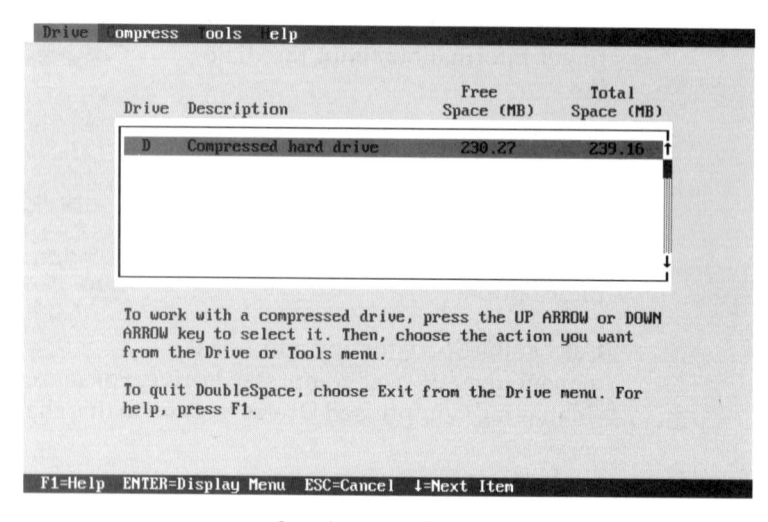

Starting DoubleSpace

DoubleSpace interface

The DoubleSpace interface conforms to the SAA/CUA standard. So, it will be familiar to you if you work with programs such as Word 6.0 or Works 3.0. At the top of the screen, you'll see a menu bar with the following menus:

To open a menu, press [Alt], followed by the first letter of the menu name. For example, pressing [Alt] + [D] opens the **Drive** menu.

DoubleSpace

Chapter Four

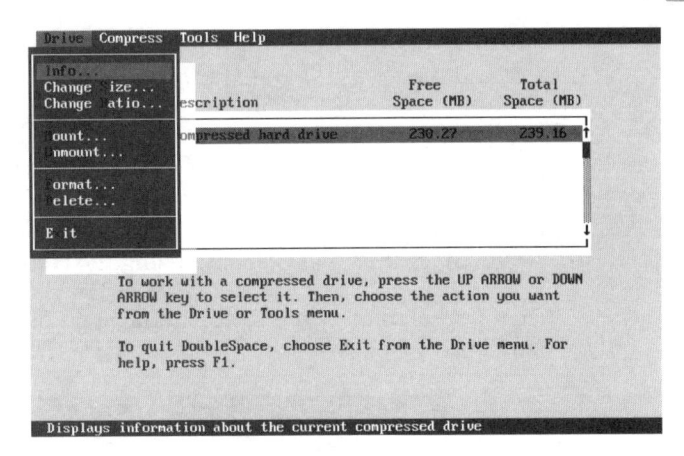

Drive menu

To choose a command from the menu, use the cursor keys and press [Enter] or press the highlighted letter in the command name. For example, press [X] to activate the Exit command. Press [Esc] to exit a menu.

Press [F1] at any time to display a help text. Use the cursor keys to browse through the text.

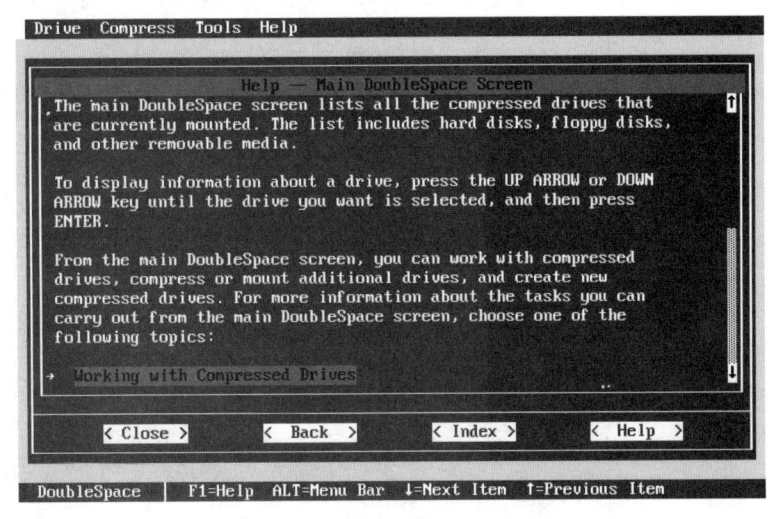

Help text

DoubleSpace

Chapter Four

Sometimes related topics appear in a different color. Press [Tab] to select the topic and then press [Enter] to jump to the next help topic.

You can also use [Tab] to move to the [Close], [Back], [Index] and [Help] buttons. Choose [Close] to exit Help and return to normal program execution. You can do the same thing by pressing [Esc]. Choose [Back] to return to the previous Help screen. [Index] displays the table of contents for Help and [Help] displays information about using the Help function itself.

When you activate some commands, such as **Options...** in the **Tools** menu, dialog boxes appear on the screen.

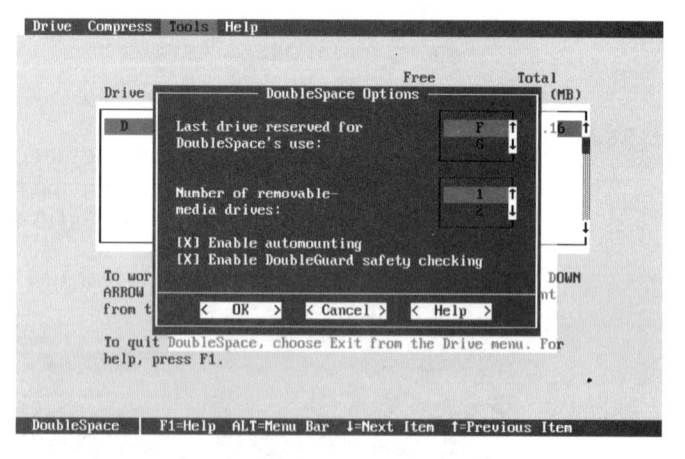

Dialog boxes

Dialog boxes contain the [OK], [Cancel], and [Help] buttons. Press [Tab] to change to a different button, and press [Enter] to activate a button. Pressing [Esc] is always the same as clicking the [Cancel] button.

The dialog boxes also contain list boxes and text boxes. Use the cursor keys to select an entry in the list boxes, and then type a number or text in the text boxes. Press [Tab] to change to a different text box or list box.

A list of the compressed drives appears in the middle of the screen. The "MB" entries refer to compressed values and are estimates based on the average compression ratio for "Free Memory." Use the cursor keys to select a drive.

DoubleSpace

Chapter Four

Now that you're familiar with the DoubleSpace interface, we'll discuss the different management functions.

Changing the drive size

It's possible to increase or decrease the size of a compressed drive. However, to increase the size of the hard drive, the host drive must have enough free memory.

DoubleSpace can help you determine whether it's possible to increase the drive. To do this, choose **Info...** in the **Drive** menu. The Info dialog box appears.

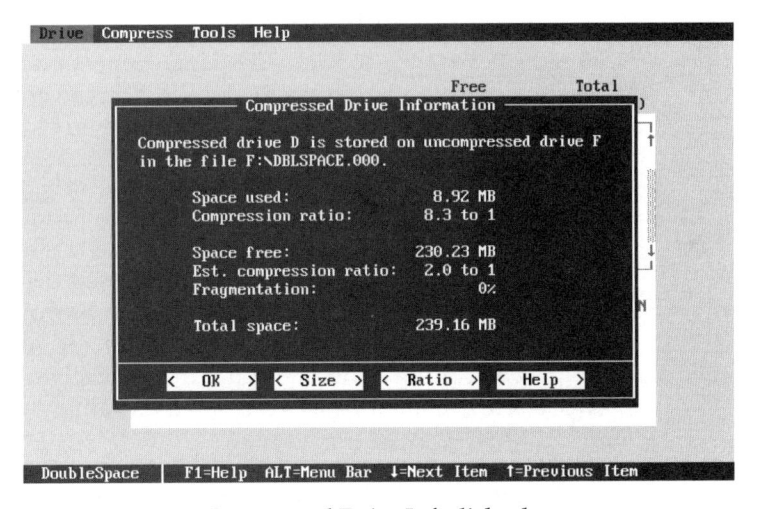

Compressed Drive Info dialog box

The dialog box provides the following information:

"Space used:"

The amount of memory allocated by the compressed drive.

"Compression ratio:"

The average compression ratio.

Chapter Four

"Space free:"

This is the amount of free memory based on the estimated compression ratio.

"Est. compression ratio:"

The estimated compression ratio for the future.

"Total space:"

Total space of the compressed drive if the estimated compression ratio turns out to be valid.

First, you can use this information to determine how much memory is still free on the compressed drive. This is an important criterion for users who decide to reduce the compressed drive. You can only reduce the drive by the amount of free space on it. Otherwise, you would destroy data.

However, you can also use the amount of free memory to determine whether it is necessary or even advisable to increase the size of the compressed drive. For example, if you intend to place graphic files, which can be tightly compressed, on a compressed drive that contains only program files, which don't compress well at all, a rough estimate can show you whether the graphic files will fit on the drive. It's possible that the improved compression rate could dramatically increase the amount of free space in comparison to the previous value.

Finally, you can also judge whether data compression has been worthwhile up to this point. Compression ratios that are far below 2 to 1 aren't worth the trouble of compressing the drive. In such cases, reduce the drive. If the value is significantly higher, you should consider giving the compressed drive more space.

Now click the Size button or choose **Change Size...** in the **Drive** menu. The "Change Size" dialog box appears.

DoubleSpace

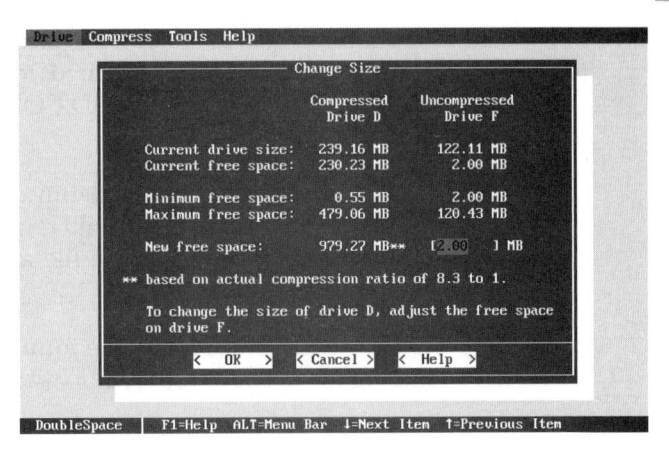

Chapter Four

Change Size dialog box

Tables illustrate the ratio of the compressed volume file and the host drive. All the values are based on an estimated compression rate of 2 to 1. The following values are given:

- The current drive size of the compressed drive indicates how much data the compressed volume file can contain at full capacity and a compression ratio of 2 to 1.

- The current drive size of the uncompressed drive indicates the actual amount of memory, in megabytes, on the physical hard drive.

- The current free space of the compressed drive shows how much more data the compressed volume file will be able to hold at the estimated compression ratio.

- The current free space of the uncompressed drive shows how much physical memory is still free. The compressed volume file could utilize this free memory.

- The "Minimum free space" specification for the compressed drive indicates how much memory is required for the DoubleSpace system.

- The "Maximum free space" entry for the compressed drive indicates how much memory the compressed volume file could provide if maximum compression were achieved for the data to be stored.

Chapter Four

- The "Minimum free space" value for the uncompressed drive describes the amount of free memory required for the DOS system files MSDOS.SYS, IO.SYS, COMMAND.COM, and the permanent Windows swap file.

- The "Maximum free space" value for the uncompressed drive describes the amount of free memory that would result if you deleted all data, except for the compressed volume file and the system data that cannot be compressed.

In the "New free space" line, specify the future size of the compressed drive by entering the desired free memory capacity at "Uncompressed drive."

If this is smaller than the current value under "Free space/Uncompressed drive", increase the compressed volume file. If you choose a larger value, the volume file will decrease in size.

Experiment with these values. If you use a value that isn't possible, the "Illegal" message appears in the "Compressed drive" column. Changes that can be performed are indicated by the "New free space" message in the "Compressed drive" column. This new memory specifies how large the compressed drive would be at a compression ratio of 2 to 1.

Now enter the desired change or cancel the dialog box. Select **Info...** in the **Drive** menu to check the effects of your new settings.

Changing the compression ratio

As you know, the specification about the amount of free space left on a compressed drive is an estimate based on the estimated compression ratio. This compression ratio is assumed at 2 to 1, so the size of a 50 Meg compressed hard drive is estimated to be 100 Meg. The actual size of the compressed hard drive mainly depends on the data stored on this drive and the actual attained compression ratio.

DoubleSpace gives you an opportunity to change the compression ratio. This doesn't mean you're changing the method of compression, which could result in a greater compression of the data. Instead, you only change the value of the compression ratio for the estimate of free space. For example, if you change the estimated compression ratio to 3 to 1, the 50

DoubleSpace

Chapter Four

Meg hard drive will increase to an estimated 150 Meg free for compression. However, if you only attain the average compression ratio of 2 to 1, the hard drive will still hold only 100 Meg of data.

As you can see, it isn't possible to make drastic changes by changing the compression ratio. However, activating **Change Ratio...** in the **Drive** menu is still helpful. We'll discuss this in detail.

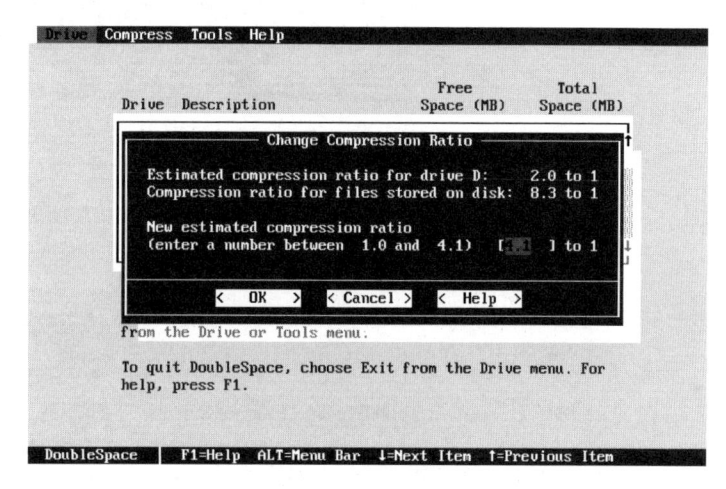

Change Ratio dialog box

This dialog box indicates on which ratio the estimate of free space is based. Enter a new ratio between 1 and 8. Lower the estimated ratio if you'll be saving only files that don't compress well. Increase the ratio if you want to store data that compresses well on the compressed hard drive, such as texts, tables, databases, and especially graphics. Refer to Chapter 2 for more information on how well specific file types compress.

Formatting compressed drives

Compressed volume files are only files on the hard drive, but you can still format the logical, compressed drives that these files represent. However, formatting a compressed drive that you've just created isn't necessary.

Select the **Format...** command in the **Drive** menu. The following dialog box appears:

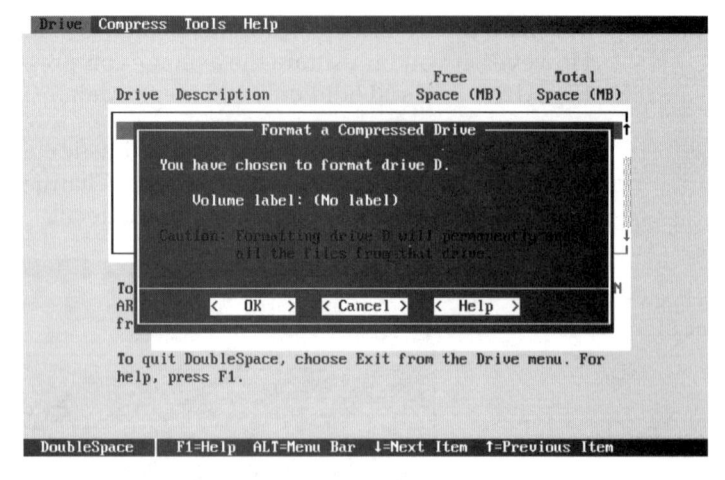

Chapter Four

Format dialog box

Choose OK to begin formatting. This deletes all the data on the drive.

Deleting compressed drives

You can also delete a compressed drive by choosing the **Delete...** command in the **Drive** menu. A dialog box appears.

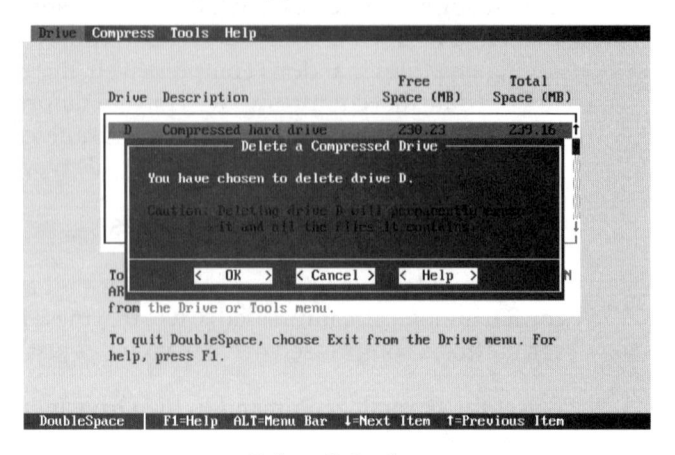

Warning
Don't format your new compressed drive. If you do this, you'll lose all the data on the drive.

Delete dialog box

DoubleSpace

Chapter Four

Confirm your choice by clicking [OK], if you're sure you want to delete the drive.

Defragmenting drives

Even compressed drives can become fragmented, so occasionally you must defragment your compressed drive. However, you cannot use the DOS utility program DEFRAG to do this. Instead, you must use a special DoubleSpace command.

> **Warning**
> When you delete a drive, you also lose all the files on this drive. Be very careful and always make sure you aren't deleting something that you still need.

Choose the **Defragment...** command from the **Tools** menu. A confirmation prompt appears, giving you a chance to change your mind about defragmenting the compressed drive. Remember that defragmenting can be time-consuming. Therefore, you may want to defragment the drive when you won't be needing your computer for awhile.

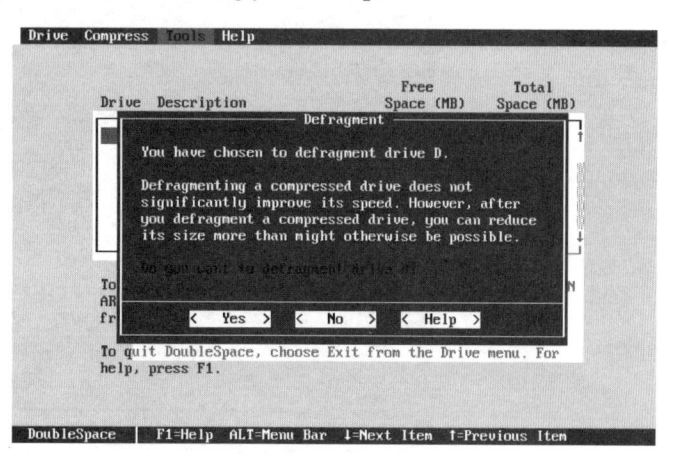

Confirmation prompt

After you confirm the prompt, the command begins defragmenting your compressed drive. A percentage bar indicates the progress.

DoubleSpace

Chapter Four

Compressing diskettes

There are various ways to exchange large amounts of data easily and quickly. Computer networks and modems are good examples of these methods. However, most computer users still use diskettes to exchange data.

DoubleSpace gives you the option of compressing diskettes, which makes it easier to send data on diskettes. Simply compress a blank diskette, then copy the data to the diskette and use a special command to load the data in the computer. The procedure is as follows:

1. Start DoubleSpace and insert the diskette you want compressed into drive A: or B:. The diskette should be blank and formatted.

2. Select **Existing Drive** from the **Compress** menu. A list of the drives that are available for compression appears.

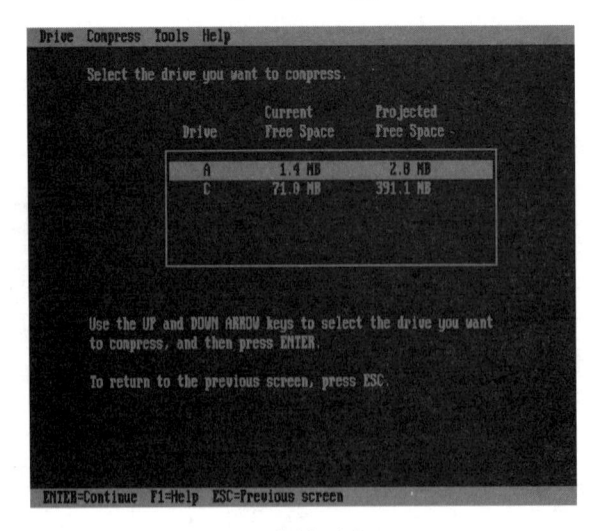

Available drives

3. Choose drive A: or B:.

4. DoubleSpace runs CHKDSK, and then compresses the diskette. The compressed diskette appears in the list of compressed drives in DoubleSpace.

DoubleSpace

Chapter Four

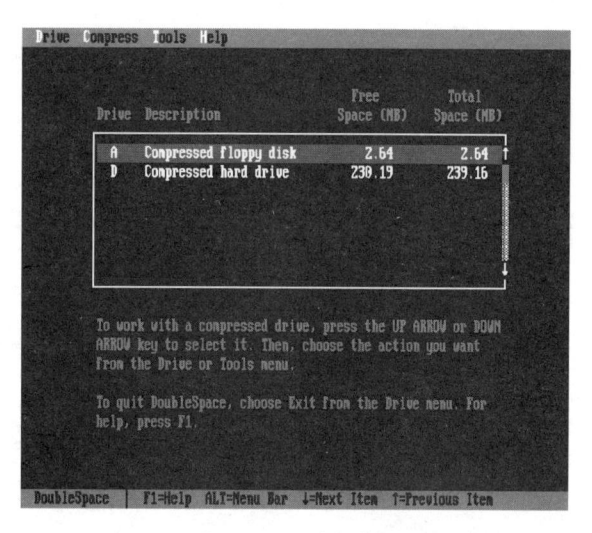

Compressed diskette

5. Exit DoubleSpace by selecting **Exit** from the **Drive** menu.

6. Save the data you want stored on the diskette. Address the compressed diskette as you would any other diskette in drive A: or B:.

Before you can insert other diskettes, you must unmount the compressed diskette. Use the following procedure to do this:

> **Note**
> An error message may appear stating that you cannot create a compressed drive. If this occurs, you may have to add an extra letter under **Options** in the **Tools** menu to "Last drive reserved for DoubleSpace's use:." Then restart your computer and start over with step 1.

1. Start DoubleSpace.

2. Select the disk drive from the list of compressed drives.

3. Select the **Unmount...** command in the **Drive** menu. A security prompt appears.

DoubleSpace

Chapter Four

Security prompt for Unmount

4. Confirm by clicking OK. Now you can insert other diskettes into drive A: or B:.

From the DOS prompt, change to the drive in which the compressed diskette is located and enter:

DBLSPACE /UNMOUNT Enter

Now the diskette is unmounted.

To read a compressed diskette, use the following procedure:

1. Insert the compressed diskette into drive A: or B:.

2. Start DoubleSpace.

3. Choose the **Mount...** command from the **Drive** menu. Then choose drive A: or B:.

> *Note*
> Mounting and unmounting isn't necessary in DOS 6.2. It has an Automount function which automatically mounts and unmounts compressed diskettes. Activate Automount in DBLSPACE.INI. We'll discuss Automount later in this chapter.

DoubleSpace

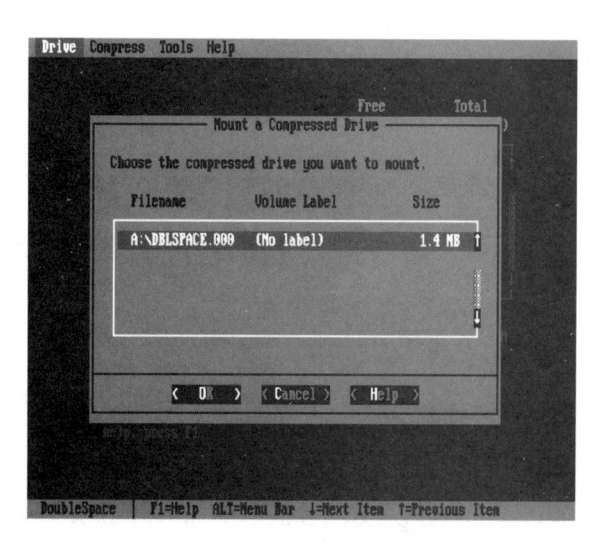

Chapter Four

Mounting a drive

4. DoubleSpace reads the diskette, displaying it in the list of compressed drives.

5. Exit DoubleSpace by selecting **Exit** in the **Drive** menu.

Now you can process the compressed diskette, like any other diskette.

From the DOS prompt, change to the drive in which the compressed diskette is located and enter:

DBLSPACE /MOUNT [Enter]

Now the diskette is mounted.

> **Note**
>
> An error message may appear stating that you cannot create a compressed drive. If this occurs, you may have to add an extra letter under **Options** in the **Tools** menu to "Last drive reserved for DoubleSpace's use:." Then restart your computer and start over with step 1.

DoubleSpace

Chapter Four

Optimizing Your Hard Drive

Ever since PCs first appeared, optimization has been important. The main purpose of optimizing, or improving the performance of your PC, is increasing the processing speed. With DoubleSpace, the size of the available hard drive disk space, the use of RAM, and access speed are important.

More space for the hard drive

Installing DoubleSpace and creating compressed drives on your system is a major part of optimizing the free disk space on your hard drive. Once you've done that, there's not much more you can do.

If you compressed only part of your hard drive, you can change the size of the compressed hard drive, thus increasing the amount of available disk space. For information on how to do this, refer to the section called "Changing the drive size."

Delete any unnecessary files. Even compressed diskettes can quickly accumulate garbage data like .TMP and .BAK files. To determine what you can delete, refer to the section called "Deleting unnecessary files."

The amount of free disk space you specify on a compressed volume depends mainly on the estimated compression ratio. In the beginning, DoubleSpace assumes a ratio of 2 to 1. Later the ratio is adjusted based on the actual compression ratio attained with the files stored on the drive.

However, if you know that the files you'll be saving in the future will produce a much better compression ratio, then you should increase the estimated compression ratio. By doing this, you also increase the amount of free disk space that's available.

We explained this procedure in the "Compression Ratios" section in Chapter 2. For more information on attainable compression ratios, refer to Chapter 2.

Finally, you can increase the amount of free disk space on the hard drive by making better use of the compressed hard drive. This is especially useful when your compression ratio has been under 2 to 1 and you still

DoubleSpace

Chapter Four

have many files stored on the uncompressed drive that will compress tightly. Move the files that compress well (tightly) to the compressed drive and move files that compress poorly from the compressed drive to the uncompressed drive. For more information on the compression ratios of various file types, refer to Chapter 2.

More free RAM

If it seems like the amount of available memory under DOS or Windows has gotten noticeably smaller or is too small for some applications that used to run, you must optimize RAM and its usage. To do this, use the MEMMAKER program, which we discussed in Chapter 3.

Also, you should remove unnecessary drivers and other memory-resident programs. If you don't know whether these drivers and programs are necessary, use the REM command in the CONFIG.SYS and AUTOEXEC.BAT files to temporarily disable drivers and programs. However, remember that you need the DBLSPACE.SYS driver, because this loads the DoubleSpace system.

Memory-resident virus monitors, delete protection programs, and desktop programs, such as Sidekick or PC Desktop from PC Tools, also aren't necessary. The DOS drivers Graftabl and Graphics don't have to be installed either. After permanently removing drivers and programs from your system, run MEMMAKER again.

Higher access speed

Obviously you want the highest possible access speed for reading data from or writing data to your compressed hard drive. However, there are limits to what you can do. If your computer is slow and your hard drive isn't very fast, you won't be able to make your PC extremely fast by using DoubleSpace.

However, by using the following tips, you can increase access speed:

- Defragment the compressed hard drive regularly. For information on how to do this, refer to "Defragmenting drives" on page 111.

- Check the structure of your compressed drive often. Refer to the section called "Checking partitions" on page 83.

Chapter Four

- Delete unnecessary files. Even your compressed drive can quickly collect unnecessary garbage, such as .TMP files, .BAK files, etc. To determine what you can delete, refer to the section called "Deleting unnecessary files."

- If you have large files that compress tightly and they take too much time for loading and saving, you may be better off with smaller files that don't compress so well. The less you have to compress, the faster you can load and save. However, by doing this, you're wasting disk space.

DBLSPACE.INF

DoubleSpace also uses initialization and system files. One of these is a file called "DBLSPACE.INF", which is located in the DOS directory. You can edit this file with the DOS Editor. First we'll show you the text of the original file and then we'll explain how to change this file.

The following is the original DBLSPACE.INF:

```
; Microsoft DoubleSpace Setup Information File
;
; This file customizes the behavior of DoubleSpace when it is compressing
; existing drives or creating new drives.
;
; Commands under [SpecialFiles] indicate actions to be taken for specific
; files; the options are COPY=filename, IGNORE=filename, and MOVE=filename.
; Without a path, any file of that name will match; wildcards (?, *) are
; acceptable.
;
; COPY=
; Specified file(s) are copied to compressed drive, and left behind on the
; uncompressed drive.
;
; IGNORE=
; Specified file(s) are left behind on the uncompressed drive.
;
; MOVE=
; Specified file(s) are moved to the compressed drive. This is the
; default behavior for all files, except those with the SYSTEM attribute.

[SpecialFiles]
;
; The following two exceptions are for Microsoft Chart, French version:
 MOVE=MC.COM
 MOVE=MCA
;
; The following two exceptions are for Microsoft Multiplan, French version:
;
 MOVE=PLAN.COM
 MOVE=MPA
```

DoubleSpace

Chapter Four

```
;
; The following two exceptions are for Microsoft Word, French version:
;
 MOVE=MW.COM
 MOVE=MWA
;
; Programs under [CopyFiles] are optional utilities that will be left on the
; original boot drive if there is enough space.
;
[CopyFiles]
 MSD.EXE
 MEM.EXE
;
; Programs under [dangerous] will be REM'ed out of config.sys during
; DoubleSpace Setup, and will be restored when Setup is complete.
;
[Dangerous]
 PROTMAN
 WORKGRP
 UBNEI
 UBXPS
 ELNKII
 INTERLNK
 MC.SYS
 FASTOPEN
;
; Programs under [prior] will have DEVICEHIGH=DBLSPACE.SYS placed before
; them in config.sys. This is done to avoid memory incompatibilities.
; Note that it is okay to have multiple DBLSPACE.SYS lines in config.sys;
; any redundant loads are ignored.
;
[Prior]
 PROTMAN
;
; [Fragments] accepts two lines: Initial=#### and Addition=####. Initial
; is the number of fragments which will be allowed during SETUP; Addition is
; the number of fragments we allow, above that which is currently in use,
; at all other times with DoubleSpace.
;
[Fragments]
 Initial=2600
 Addition=110
;
[UncompressSpecial]
DONTCOPY=DBLSPACE.INI
DONTCOPY=DBLSPACE.BIN
```

And now the explanations:

`; COPY=filename`

specifies files to be copied to the compressed drive during installation of a DoubleSpace drive.

`; IGNORE=filename`

Chapter Four

specifies files to be left on the uncompressed part of the hard drive when you set up a compressed drive. Such files include the DOS system files MSDOS.SYS, IO.SYS, and COMMAND.COM as well as the Windows swap file. (DoubleSpace takes care of this even if you don't make the appropriate Ignore entries.)

```
; MOVE=filename
```

specifies files to be moved to the new compressed hard drive. For example, you could automatically move all image files, since they give the greatest gain when you compress them.

```
[SpecialFiles]
```

lists special cases such as the French program versions of Chart, Multiplan, and Word and determines what happens to specific program files.

```
[CopyFiles]
MSD.EXE
MEM.EXE
```

lists files and programs that should also be left as copies on the host drive, if possible.

```
[Dangerous]
PROTMAN
WORKGRP
UBNEI
UBXPS
ELNKII
INTERLNK
MC.SYS
FASTOPEN
```

lists programs that could cause problems when you install DoubleSpace and will not be called during Setup from the AUTOEXEC.BAT and CONFIG.SYS files.

```
[Prior]
PROTMAN
```

lists programs that should be called in CONFIG.SYS rather than DBLSPACE.SYS. This prevents incompatibilities.

DoubleSpace

Chapter Four

```
[Fragments]
  Initial=2600
  Addition=110
```

Initial specifies the number of fragments that will be allowed during installation of DoubleSpace. The value of Addition is added to Initial when DoubleSpace begins working. In the example, there can be no more than 2600 fragments, but with the Addition added 2710 are possible.

DBLSPACE.INI

There is a hidden file in the root directory called "DBLSPACE.INI." You can also edit this file with the DOS Editor, after clearing the System, Hidden and Read-Only attributes of the file, but you should handle this file carefully. First we'll show you the original file:

```
MaxRemovableDrives=2
FirstDrive=D
LastDrive=E
MaxFileFragments=112
ActivateDrive=D,C1
```

Now we'll explain the contents of this file:

`MaxRemovableDrives=2`

Specifies the number of disk drives. It can be set in DoubleSpace by selecting **Options...** from the **Tools** menu.

`FirstDrive=D`

Specifies the drive letter of the first free drive for DoubleSpace. The first compressed drive could have this letter.

`LastDrive=E`

Specifies the last drive letter that can be used by DoubleSpace. It can be changed in DoubleSpace by choosing **Options...** from the **Tools** menu.

`MaxFileFragments=112`

Specifies the maximum number of file fragments allowed within a file.

Chapter Four

```
ActivateDrive=D,C1
```

Specifies compressed drives to be loaded automatically during system startup. In the example, the compressed hard drive D: is loaded, which is located on the host drive, C: in the compressed volume file DBLSPACE.001.

DOS 6.2 Additions

In DOS 6.2 some commands have been added to DBLSPACE.INI. These commands are entered at the DOS prompt. You can change the contents of the file without editing the file.

Syntax:

```
DBLSPACE /AUTOMOUNT=0|1|A...Z
```

Enables or disables DoubleSpace 6.2's ability to automatically mount and unmount compressed diskettes. A setting of 0 disables the Automount function, which saves memory. 1 enables the Automount function, and is the default setting. A..Z specifies the drive to be mounted automatically.

```
DBLSPACE /DOUBLEGUARD=0|1
```

Enables or disables the DoubleGuard function. 0 switches DoubleGuard off, while 1 switches the function on. 1 is the default setting.

```
DLBSPACE /LASTDRIVE=x
```

Specifies the last drive letter for DoubleSpace with x.

```
DBLSPACE /MAXFILEFRAGMENTS=n
```

Specifies the maximum number of file fragments allowed with n.

```
DBLSPACE /MAXREMOVABLEDRIVES=n
```

Specifies the maximum number of compressed drives with n.

DoubleSpace

Chapter Four

```
DBLSPACE /ROMSERVER=0|1_
```

Enables or disables the ROM BIOS real time compression system of Microsoft (Microsoft Real-time Compression Interface MRCI). 0 disables the function, while 1 enables the function. However, use the ROM server only if you're using hardware that supports MRCI.

```
DBLSPACE /SWITCHES=F|N|FN_
```

You can exclude DoubleSpace 6.2 from starting when you start up the system by pressing [F5] or [F8] when the "Starting MS-DOS..." prompt appears. You will be asked to confirm each line in your AUTOEXEC.BAT and CONFIG.SYS file. By answering "N" to a prompt, you can skip any line in the files.

This can give you a system environment without DoubleSpace. This can be useful for system checks, memory-intensive applications, etc.

N increases the speed of startup by shortening the time in which you may cancel startup.

F prevents you from cancelling startup of DoubleSpace. However, you can still use [Ctrl] + [F8] to select commands in the CONFIG.SYS and AUTOEXEC.BAT files and still bypass both start files with [Ctrl] + [F5]. However, DoubleSpace is still activated.

FN combines the effects of both switches.

```
DBLSPACE drive1:/HOST=drive2_
```

Changes the drive letter of the host drive. drive1 specifies the current letter, while drive2 specifies the new letter.

DoubleSpace and Other Applications

DoubleSpace is usually compatible with your applications. You can eliminate any possible incompatibilities by updating to the latest version of the applications you're using, since most software companies ensure

Chapter Four

that their products are compatible with DoubleSpace. After all, DoubleSpace is an integral part of the operating system beginning with DOS 6.0.

However, occasionally you must create compatibility by using a trick or some special precautions. We'll discuss these special cases in this section.

Cache programs

Not all cache programs are compatible with DoubleSpace. For example, DoubleSpace Setup may indicate that your computer is running an incompatible cache program. Do the following to avoid this error message:

1. Open your CONFIG.SYS and AUTOEXEC.BAT system files and delete the line containing the command that loads your hard drive cache program.

2. Make sure you add a line that calls the MS-DOS 6 SMARTDRV program. For example, if your MS-DOS directory is C:\DOS, add the following line:

    ```
    C:\DOS\SMARTDRV.EXE
    ```

3. Save the file and reboot your computer by pressing [Ctrl] + [Alt] + [Del]. Then run DoubleSpace again.

Windows swap file

For technical reasons, the permanent Windows swap file cannot be on a compressed drive. The Windows Control Panel will allow you to create the swap file on a compressed drive. Unfortunately, when you install DoubleSpace, the swap file is automatically moved to the uncompressed part of the hard drive.

If your permanent Windows swap file is on a compressed drive, Windows displays the message "The permanent swap file is corrupt" at startup. Here's how you can solve this problem:

1. Start Windows.

2. In the "Permanent swap file corrupt" dialog box, answer the question "Do you want to delete this swap file?" with Y and press [Enter].

DoubleSpace

Chapter Four

3. After Windows starts, open the Control Panel and double-click the 386 Enhanced icon.

4. Click the [Virtual Memory] button. Windows displays a dialog box informing you that a corrupt swap file has been found, and asks whether you want to set the file length to zero.

5. Click [Yes]. Windows displays another dialog box, called "Virtual Memory."

6. Click the [Change] button. Windows displays the settings of the swap file.

7. In the "Drive" list box, choose a drive that isn't compressed. In the "Type" list box, choose the option "Permanent."

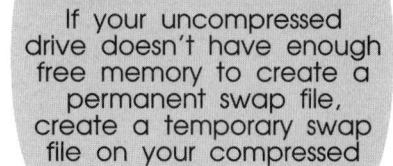

> **Note**
> If your uncompressed drive doesn't have enough free memory to create a permanent swap file, create a temporary swap file on your compressed or uncompressed drive.

8. After you've made the settings, click [OK] twice. Windows displays a dialog box that prompts you to restart Windows.

9. Click the [Restart Windows] button.

EXTDISK.SYS device driver

If you use DoubleSpace and the EXTDISK.SYS device driver is loaded in your CONFIG.SYS file, EXTDISK.SYS displays the following message when it loads:

"WARNING: EXTDISK.SYS is not the first device driver to assign drive letters. Physical hard drive letters will not be contiguous."

> **Note**
> EXTDISK.SYS displays this message regardless of where the DBLSPACE.SYS device driver is loaded in the CONFIG.SYS.

However, the EXTDISK.SYS driver works properly despite this message. This message appears only because EXTDISK.SYS is usually the first device driver to assign drive letters. Since DBLSPACE.BIN loads before the CONFIG.SYS file and assigns some drive letters, EXTDISK.SYS is no longer first.

Drive device driver

If you need a special device driver to use a drive such as a tape drive, you can still use DoubleSpace to compress this drive. However, DoubleSpace won't recognize this drive automatically, since it isn't physically present at system startup.

To tell DoubleSpace to load a compressed drive that requires a specific device driver, add the DBLSPACE /MOUNT command for this drive to the beginning of your AUTOEXEC.BAT file. For example, if drive D: needs the device driver, add the following command to the beginning of your AUTOEXEC.BAT file:

```
DBLSPACE /MOUNT D:
```

Compressed files

Some files (for example, .ZIP, .ARC, and hard drive files) are already compressed. DoubleSpace may not be able to compress these files again.

Encrypted data files, such as .MMF files of Microsoft Mail 3.0, cannot be compressed either. These files are saved in uncompressed form, even if you store them on a compressed drive.

It's better to store uncompressed files on a drive that isn't compressed. This can increase the speed of your system.

Windows NT Flexboot System

Don't compress the BOOT.INI, BOOTSECT.DOS, NTLDR, and NTDETECT.COM files of Windows NT. Add these files to the DBLSPACE.INF file in the [SpecialFiles] section before starting DoubleSpace. For more information on DBLSPACE.INF, refer to the section "Optimizing Your Hard Drive" in this chapter.

DoubleSpace

Chapter Four

Novell networks

When you load NETX.COM, you establish a network drive connection. To do this, the drive letter specified in the LASTDRIVE command of your CONFIG.SYS file is used. This also applies to the following files:

- NET5.COM
- BNETX.COM
- BNETX.EXE
- XMSNET5.EXE
- XMSNETX.EXE
- EMSNET5.EXE
- EMSNETX.EXE

If you don't specify a LASTDRIVE, MS-DOS uses "E" as a default, so your network software uses "F" when you connect to the network.

By default, DoubleSpace reserves four drive letters between the local compressed drive and the host drive for the compressed volume file (CVF). These drive letters are reserved for later use by a RAM drive, ROM drive, or a second hard drive. This can result in a drive letter conflict if you compress your local drive.

For example, if you have a logical partition on your hard drive called C: and you compress drive C:, DoubleSpace reserves drive letters "D:" to "G:" for later use and "H:" for the drive that receives the CVF. If you don't specify a LASTDRIVE command, your network software uses the drive letter that comes after the host drive, which in this case would be "I:". In your AUTOEXEC.BAT file or the batch file you use to log onto the network, all commands that assume that the network drive has a different drive letter will cause problems. There are two ways to avoid drive conflicts:

1. When you install DoubleSpace, choose **Custom setup**. Then specify a letter for your host drive that won't cause any conflicts with the letter for your network software. If your network drive is currently "F:", you could use "E:" as a drive label when you install DoubleSpace.

DoubleSpace

Chapter Four

2. Change the drive references in your AUTOEXEC.BAT file or in the batch file you use to log onto the network. Ensure that, after you install DoubleSpace, the references to drive letters match the letters that your network software uses by default. If you log on manually, use a drive letter that follows the letter that DoubleSpace uses for the compressed drive.

DOS DEFRAG

You can use the DOS Defragmenter or another defragmenting program to defragment your compressed or uncompressed drives, if you don't change the file attributes of your compressed volume files. If you change the attributes of the compressed drive and defragment your uncompressed drive, you could lose data.

Common Error Messages

Although you may encounter problems while using DoubleSpace, usually these problems are easily solved. In this section, we'll discuss some common error messages and show you how to eliminate them.

The compressed drive does not have enough disk space

If your compressed drive no longer has enough disk space, you can use one of the following methods to make more disk space available:

- Increase the size of the drive (see the "Managing Compressed Drives" section in this chapter).

- Specify a higher expected compression ratio for the drive (see the "Managing Compressed Drives" section in this chapter).

- Run the DBLSPACE /DEFRAG /F and DBLSPACE /DEFRAG commands for the drive (see Chapter 6).

> **Note**
> Sometimes you can free up additional space on a compressed drive by having DoubleSpace defragment the drive twice: Once with and once without the /F switch.

DoubleSpace

Chapter Four

The uncompressed drive does not have enough disk space

If your uncompressed drive (host drive) no longer has enough disk space, you can increase its size by reducing the size of the compressed drive(s) stored on the uncompressed drive. Naturally, this also reduces the amount of free memory on the compressed drive(s). For more information, refer to the "Managing Compressed Drives" section in this chapter.

DoubleSpace doesn't compress all the files, because enough disk space isn't available

If DoubleSpace indicates that it couldn't compress some of your files because there isn't enough available disk space, do the following:

1. Back up the files that are still uncompressed on the host drive to diskettes.
2. Now delete those uncompressed files from the host drive.
3. Enter "DBLSPACE" at the DOS prompt.
4. Now select **Change Size...** from the **Drive** menu.
5. To increase the size of your compressed drive, reduce the size of your host drive.
6. Choose **Exit** from the **Drive** menu.
7. Now copy the backed up files back to your host drive.

The Defragmenter runs out of memory while you're compressing a drive

If the Defragmenter runs out of memory while you're compressing a drive, use MEMMAKER to optimize the memory. (Refer to Chapter 3 for more information.)

If you still don't have enough memory after running MEMMAKER, there may be too many files on your hard drive, which prevents the Defragmenter from reorganizing them. You may have to delete some files in order for the program to run properly. To determine which files you can delete, refer to the section called "Deleting unnecessary files."

Chapter Four

DoubleSpace displays the message "Drive X is too fragmented to resize"

You probably have files with the Read-only file attribute on your compressed drive. These files prevent DEFRAG from optimizing your hard drive.

To solve this problem, do the following:

1. Change to the drive specified by DoubleSpace in the message.

2. To find the Read-only files, enter the following at the DOS prompt:

   `DIR /S /A:R | MORE` [Enter]

3. For each file displayed with DIR, enter

   `ATTRIB -R filename` [Enter]

   at the DOS prompt to cancel the attribute.

4. Start DEFRAG again by entering the following:

   `DEFRAG /Q /F Drive:` [Enter]

Now change the size of the DoubleSpace drive. Restore the Read-only attribute only when necessary.

The compressed drive is too large

The maximum size of a DoubleSpace-compressed drive is 512 Meg. For example, if you have a 300 Meg hard drive, the memory capacity of the hard drive after being compressed with DoubleSpace cannot be greater than 512 Meg. Either divide the hard drive into two drives of 250 Meg each, or compress only part of the hard drive.

DoubleSpace displays the message "A CVF is damaged"

If the message, "A CVF is damaged", appears after you start your computer, this means that DoubleSpace has detected a problem with a compressed volume file. Usually you'll see this message when there are cross-linked files on the compressed drive. DoubleSpace detects a cross-linked file when two files or directories are entered for the same disk space in the DoubleSpace file allocation table.

DoubleSpace

Chapter Four

You can eliminate this problem by checking the compressed hard drive. For more information, refer to the "Managing Compressed Drives" section in this chapter.

Removing DoubleSpace

Perhaps you're wondering why we would discuss removing DoubleSpace in a book that discusses the advantages of data compression. However, eventually, you may want to do this for some reason.

There is no method for automatically removing DoubleSpace. Instead, you must remove it manually, by following these steps:

1. Back up the files on the compressed drive. If you use a backup program, its program files must be on a different drive or on a diskette.

2. Enter "DBLSPACE /LIST" at the DOS prompt. Determine on which uncompressed drive the compressed drive is stored.

3. Copy the COMMAND.COM file from the compressed drive to the root directory of your uncompressed drive, if necessary.

4. To delete your DoubleSpace files, make your uncompressed drive the current drive. Now enter the following at the DOS prompt:

    ```
    DELTREE DBLSPACE.* Enter
    ```

    To delete only one of your DoubleSpace drives, use the DELTREE command to delete the compressed volume file for the drive. Enter the following at the command prompt:

    ```
    DELTREE DBLSPACE.000 Enter
    ```

5. Reboot your computer by pressing Ctrl + Alt + Del.

6. Restore your backup files. Naturally, this is only possible if there is enough room on the uncompressed hard drive for all of your data.

Chapter Four

You have removed DoubleSpace from your system and have a backup of your compressed data. You probably won't be able to copy all the data back to the hard drive. After all, the data was compressed, so it only took up half the space.

Uncompressing Drives (DOS 6.2)

In the DoubleSpace version for DOS 6.2, the **Tools** menu has an **Uncompress...** command. You can use this command to convert compressed drives back to uncompressed drives.

However, there is a catch. If you've filled up the entire compressed drive, it probably contains more data than will fit on the free space of the hard drive in uncompressed form. In other words, you can't really uncompress the drive unless you first reduce the amount of data on the compressed drive.

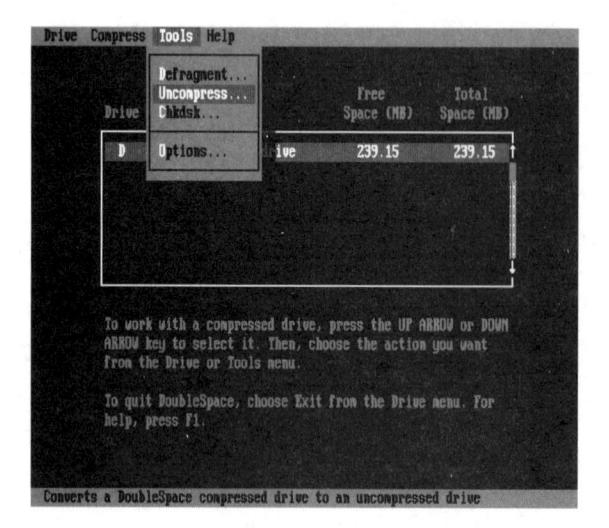

Uncompressing a drive

Chapter 5

Stacker 3.1

Contents

Installing Stacker 135

Using Compressed Drives 152

Managing Compressed Drives 157

Optimizing the Hard Drive 175

Stacker and Other Applications 179

Common Error Messages 181

Removing Stacker 183

Uncompressing Drives 184

Stacker Command Lines 185

Stacker 3.1

Chapter Five

In this chapter, we'll discuss Stacker 3.1. We'll explain how to install Stacker and how to use it to manage compressed drives. Stacker is sometimes included with OS/2 and is also used with Novell DOS. In addition, Stacker runs on all DOS versions including DOS 6, so it can be used instead of DoubleSpace.

Installing Stacker

Installing a compressed drive with Stacker is more complicated than installing standard software. After all, direct on-line compression of a drive represents quite a disruption of your system and requires the proper preparation.

> **Note**
> Before installing Stacker, read Chapter 3. Also, you should be very familiar with the FDISK, FORMAT, CHKDSK, BACKUP, RESTORE and MEMMAKER programs. Otherwise, you won't be able to install Stacker properly.

Start your computer and exit all interfaces, such as the DOS Shell or Windows, until you are at the DOS prompt. You can only install Stacker and prepare your hard drive safely and quickly at the DOS prompt.

Checking partitions

First, check the number and type of existing partitions. Since you'll install at least one more drive with Stacker, you must delete any additional logical drives created by DOS partitions. Otherwise, you'll have too many drive labels. To check the partitions, start the FDISK utility program.

Chapter Five

Checking the partitions

If you have only a primary DOS partition, everything is fine. You can exit FDISK and move on to the next step.

Use FDISK to delete any other unnecessary partitions. If you also work with IBM's OS/2 operating system, you need an OS/2 partition. If you're using SpeedStor, this program will also require a special partition. Besides these two exceptions, you should delete any partitions that you don't need.

However, when you delete partitions, you have a problem because you cannot simply add the resulting free disk space to the first primary DOS partition. It's not possible to change the partition sizes afterwards. Therefore, you must first delete all the partitions and then create a single new partition.

Since deleting a partition also means losing the data that was on the partition, you must perform a complete backup of your hard drive before deleting the partitions. Otherwise, you'll lose all your data when you repartition your hard drive.

After you finish repartitioning your hard drive, reformat the hard drive and copy the data back to the hard drive. Then you're ready for the next step.

Stacker 3.1

Chapter Five

Deleting unnecessary files

Creating a compressed drive shouldn't be like moving to a larger house. You don't have to hoard everything, even if you do have a lot of space. Therefore, don't hesitate to delete any files and programs that you never use. If you don't think you have anything that fits this description on your system, take a good look at your hard drive.

Remember that files with the following extensions are unnecessary and must be deleted before you compress your hard drive:

TMP	Temporary files
CHK	Files created by CHKDSK or SCANDSK
BAK	Program backup files
OLD	Older versions of files

DOS and Windows also come with many useless files.

Sample BASIC programs

For example, have you ever worked with QBasic and taken a look at the sample programs, such as GORILLA.BAS? If you haven't used these programs, then delete all the .BAS BASIC files in your DOS directory.

BMP wallpaper files

Do you use all the BMP wallpaper files in Windows? If not, delete the ones you don't need.

DOS Shell

If you never use the DOS Shell and prefer PC Tools, Norton Commander, or Windows, then delete the DOS Shell. The following command removes all partial programs of the Shell:

```
ERASE DOSSHELL.* Enter
```

Chapter Five

Laptop files

If you're not running DOS on a laptop, then you don't need POWER.EXE, INTERLNK.*, and INTERSVR.* either. Delete these files.

DOS utility programs

Several DOS utility programs may also be unnecessary. For example, have you ever used ATTRIB, CHCP, CTTY, DEBUG, DISKCOMP, EDIT (DOS text editor), EXPAND, FASTOPEN, FC, GRAPHICS, MSCDEX, MSD, NLSFUNC, PRINT, QBASIC, SORT, SYS, or VERIFY? If you rarely use these programs, simply move them to a backup diskette and them delete them from your hard drive.

Extensive help systems

Many application programs include extensive help systems. If you're already thoroughly familiar with an application, you probably don't use its help feature very often. In this case, delete the help files you don't need. You'll save a few megabytes (almost 2 Meg for Excel help, 1 Meg for WinWord help, 4 Meg for Access help).

Sample database files

Today, sample databases are also quite large. If you removed, for example, all the sample files of FoxPro for Windows, you would reduce the disk space required for FoxPro by half.

Dictionaries and thesauruses

Finally, many dictionaries and thesauruses are extremely large. Although these are important tools for word processing, you may not use them regularly. If you can do without your thesauruses and dictionaries, delete the directory files with the .THS and .LEX extensions.

This also applies to grammar checkers. If you eliminate these files, you'll gain a couple megabytes of free disk space. However, you will need to weigh the consequences of this action. Is the free storage space worth the loss of these valuable tools?

Stacker 3.1

Chapter Five

Since it's only possible to create compressed drives when the hard drive has at least some free memory, you need to take this step (cleaning out your hard drive) of the process seriously.

Also, creating a compressed drive on a hard drive with allocated memory is time-consuming. Therefore, it's better to compress memory that is already free. Get as much free disk space on your hard drive as you possibly can. The more free disk space, the larger your new compressed drive can be.

Removing CHK files

The second step is only applicable to systems running versions earlier than DOS 6 and requires removing all the lost clusters from the hard drive you're compressing. Systems running DOS 6 may use SCANDISK for this purpose.

To do this, activate the DOS CHKDSK utility program with the /F switch. Then use **Delete** to remove the .CHK files.

CHKDSK is used not only for compression, but also for defragmenting the hard drive.

Defragmenting

Now you're ready to defragment the hard drive. With DOS 5.0 and earlier versions, you must use one of the utility programs from PC Tools (COMPRESS) or Norton Utilities (DEFRAG). DOS 6 includes its own defragmenting program called Defrag.

Activate DEFRAG and select the recommended optimization.

Chapter Five

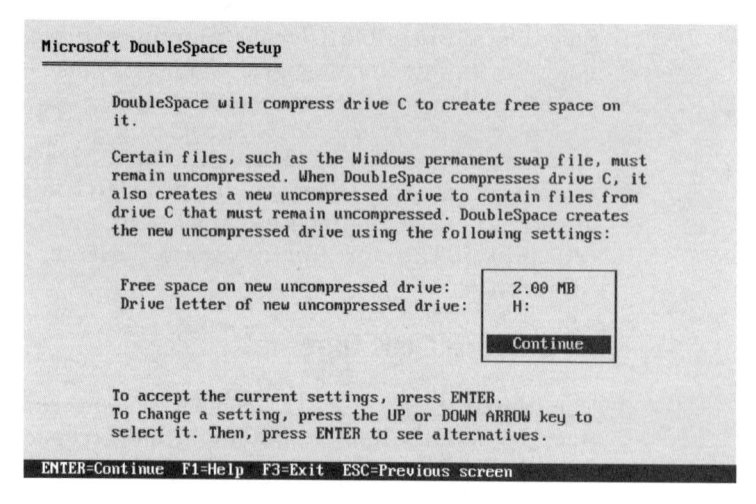

```
Microsoft DoubleSpace Setup

   DoubleSpace will compress drive C to create free space on
   it.

   Certain files, such as the Windows permanent swap file, must
   remain uncompressed. When DoubleSpace compresses drive C, it
   also creates a new uncompressed drive to contain files from
   drive C that must remain uncompressed. DoubleSpace creates
   the new uncompressed drive using the following settings:

      Free space on new uncompressed drive:    2.00 MB
      Drive letter of new uncompressed drive:  H:
                                              [ Continue ]

   To accept the current settings, press ENTER.
   To change a setting, press the UP or DOWN ARROW key to
   select it. Then, press ENTER to see alternatives.

ENTER=Continue  F1=Help  F3=Exit  ESC=Previous screen
```

Defragmenting the hard drive

Installing a compressed drive works much better on an optimized hard drive than it does on a hard drive that hasn't been optimized. After running CHKDSK and DEFRAG, reboot your computer.

Starting the installation

Stacker provides several kinds of installation. So before you begin, you must determine which type of installation is best for your system.

Important considerations

When you compress your hard drive, you want to gain as much disk space as possible in the shortest amount of time.

Some file types, such as database, text, and graphic files, compress better than other file types. These file types contain much information that is redundant, so it's easy to reduce their size. However, you don't waste much time compressing and decompressing, because, except for databases, such files are usually relatively small. Therefore, write and read operations are fast.

With databases, the entire file isn't usually affected by read or write operations. Instead, only a group of data records is affected, so compression doesn't take long with databases either.

Stacker 3.1

Chapter Five

However, generally the contents of a hard drive don't consist of just databases, texts, and graphics. The data mainly consists of programs. For example, while this book takes up only about half a Meg of disk space, the word processor we used to create and format the book requires almost six megabytes.

Programs can't be compressed very much, and the time spent compressing them needlessly slows down the execution of the applications. Therefore, you shouldn't compress program files at all.

Besides, there are some program and system files that you can't compress if you want to keep your system running. Among these files are COMMAND.COM, IO.SYS, and MSDOS.SYS, as well as the permanent Windows swap file. Therefore, you'll never be able to compress the entire hard drive. At least 1.7 Meg must be kept free on your startup drive.

Also, you should always keep some free, uncompressed memory available on your hard drive for emergencies. For example, you may want to install a program that can't work with a compressed hard drive. Or perhaps you have documents or databases that are so large, they take too much time to compress.

Now, let's review what we've learned: 1) Compress only document files. 2) Never compress your entire hard drive. As a result, we don't recommend using Express Setup when you install Stacker, because Express Setup tries to compress as much of your hard drive as possible.

Custom Setup lets you either stack the entire drive or create a drive from free space.

When you choose the first option, Stacker compresses the C: hard drive, including all of its files. The last two megabytes of the hard drive aren't compressed and are configured as drive D:. All the files that cannot be compressed are copied to this new D: drive. The compressed STACVOL file becomes part of drive D:. Drive D: becomes the new startup drive.

With the second option, Stacker first creates a new D: drive with the free disk space on drive C:. Then Stacker compresses drive D:. Other than that, nothing else changes.

Chapter Five

We recommend using the second option for two reasons: 1) You don't have to make any adjustments in using the program and the system. After all, drive C: is still drive C: and all your programs and system files remain on this drive. 2) You decide which files to move to the compressed drive. This way, you can compress only those files that can be compressed tightly.

The disadvantage of this option is that Stacker can use only the free disk space on the hard drive to create a new, compressed drive. So you need to free up as much memory as possible before using Stacker (refer to the "Deleting unnecessary files" information beginning on page 137).

However, there's another alternative: First create the compressed drive at the maximum size. Then move files from drive C:, which is uncompressed, to the compressed drive, D:. This saves you disk space, because usually compressed files on D: take up only half the memory of drive C:. So drive C: has free memory again.

Then you can use Stacker to add the free memory on C: to the compressed drive. By doing this, you can compensate for the disadvantage of using the second option.

Now let's install Stacker according to the method we discussed.

1. Activate the Stacker installation program at the DOS prompt by entering:

    A:SETUP [Enter]

2. A welcome screen appears; simply click [Continue].

Stacker 3.1

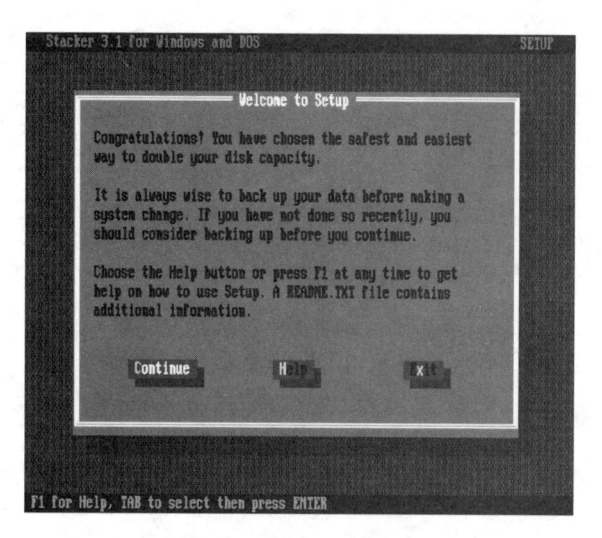

Chapter Five

Stacker Welcome Screen

3. A new screen appears, prompting you to specify your name and company. Follow the instructions on the screen.

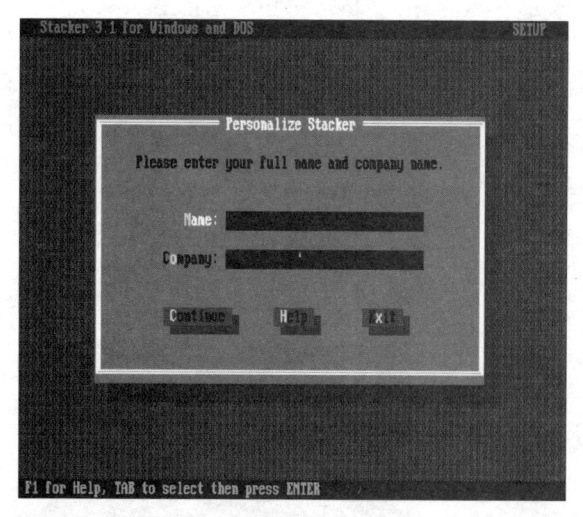

   Enter your name and company.

4. Now a dialog box appears, in which you can choose either Custom or Express Setup. Choose **Custom Setup**.

Chapter Five

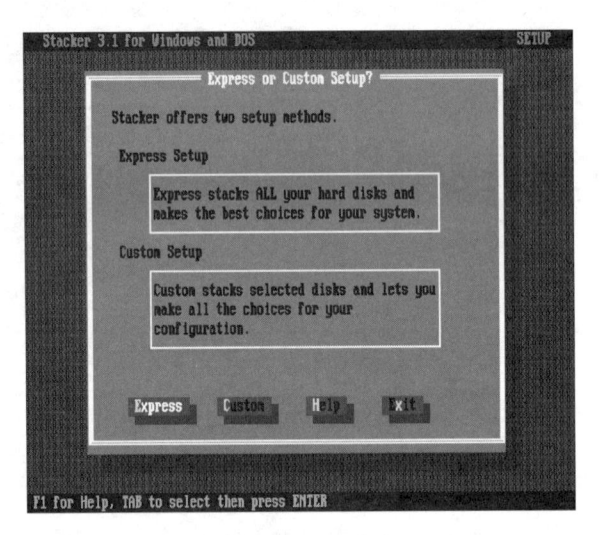

Select Custom Setup

5. Stacker recommends "C:\STACKER" as the installation directory. However, you should change the directory to "C:\DOS." By doing this, the Stacker files will be managed as a part of the operating system. Then confirm your choice with [Continue].

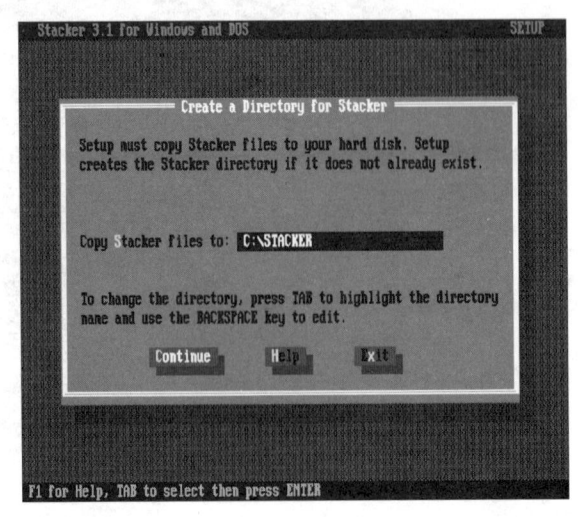

Selecting the directory for installing the Stacker files

Stacker 3.1

Chapter Five

6. Stacker gives you the option of adding the program directory to the DOS path specifications. This is useful if you want the Stacker Tools to be available always, like all DOS utility programs. However, if you place Stacker in the DOS directory as we recommended, an additional path isn't necessary.

7. Next, SETUP copies files from the Setup diskettes to your hard drive.

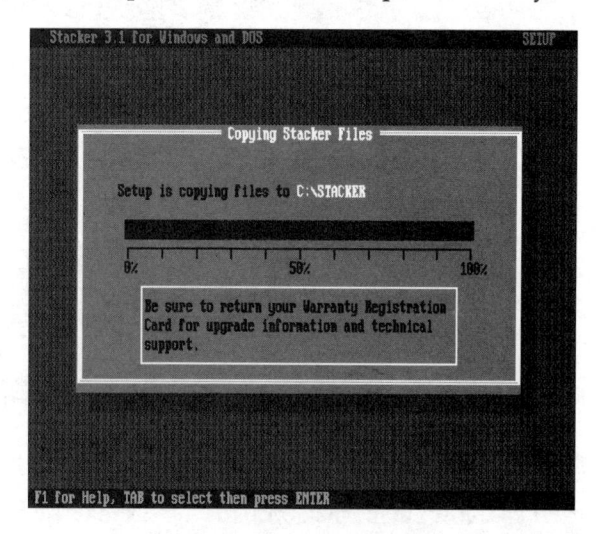

Copying the Stacker files

8. Then the Tune Stacker screen appears in which you determine how Stacker will work:

Fastest speed and standard compression

This option gives you normal compression at high speed. Choose this option if you use a slow computer (i.e., a 286).

More compression and a bit less speed

This option increases the compression ratio while maintaining the high speed in accessing the compressed data. On normal (i.e., 386) computers, choose this option.

Chapter Five

Best compression

This option gives you the best possible compression at a lower speed. This option should be used with high-speed 486 and 586 computers, since these computers are so fast.

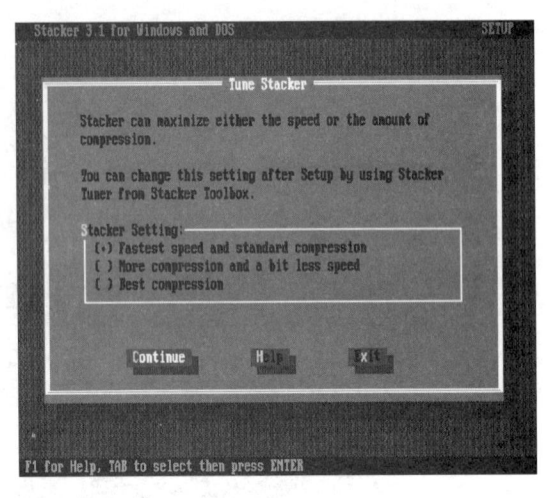

Tuning Stacker

9. Now Stacker asks you to restart the system to continue the installation under optimum conditions.

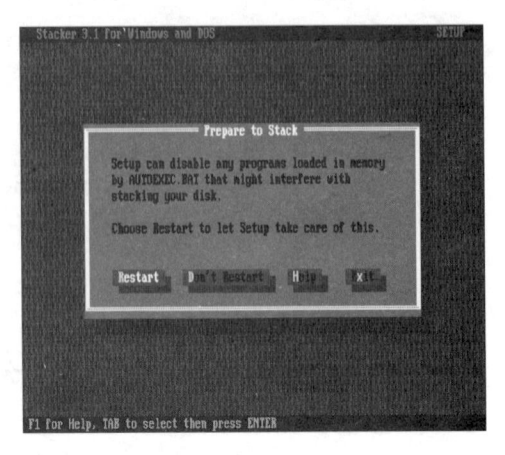

Restart your system

Stacker 3.1

Chapter Five

10. A list of available drives appears. Choose the drive (host drive) you want to provide the disk space for the compressed STACVOL file.

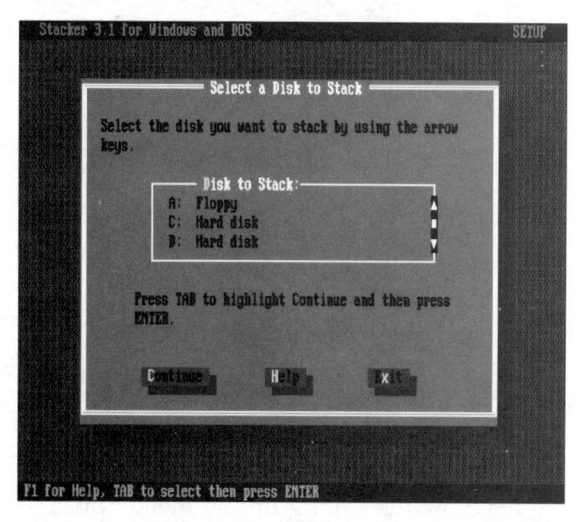

Selecting the Stacker Drive

11. Another menu appears, in which you have to choose between compressing the entire drive (Stack entire drive) and creating a new compressed drive (Create Drive from free space). Choose **Free Space**.

Stacker 3.1

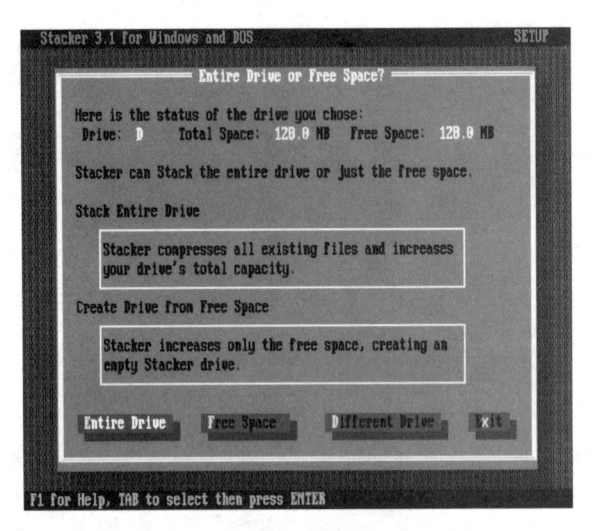

Chapter Five

Selecting the method of compression

12. Now the Configuration menu appears. Here you can choose how much free memory will be left on the host drive after creating the compressed drive or how much memory you want to use for the compressed drive.

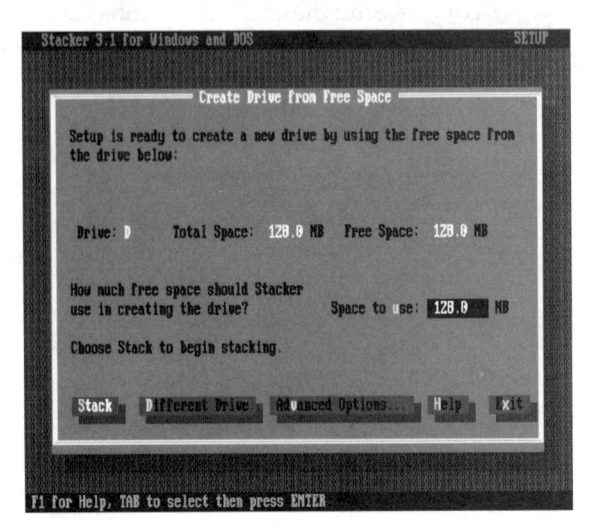

Configuration menu

Stacker 3.1

Chapter Five

13. Click [Advanced Options] to make additional settings. The "Advanced Options" screen appears.

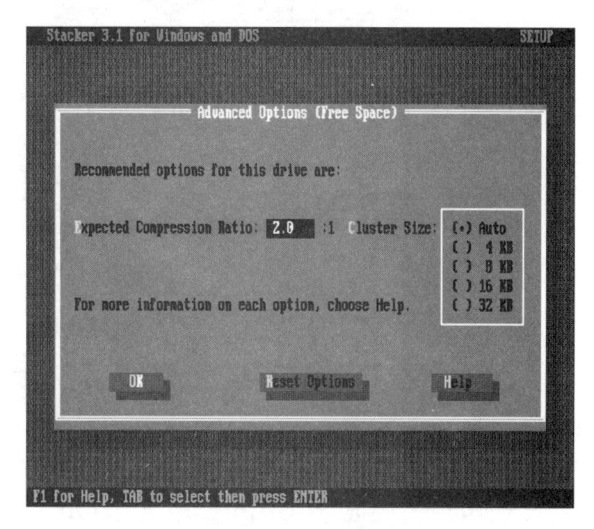

Advanced options

14. You determine the expected compression ratio in the "Advanced Options" screen. Leave this ratio set to "2 to 1", since this is the actual expected compression ratio. Adjust the Cluster Size to the expected average file size on the compressed drive. The smaller the files, the smaller the cluster size. For drives that will provide more than 512 Meg of free disk space after compression, only 32K clusters are possible.

15. Click [OK] and then activate the [Stack] button. Stacker creates a new, compressed drive on the selected drive.

16. Choose **Restart** to restart your computer.

Chapter Five

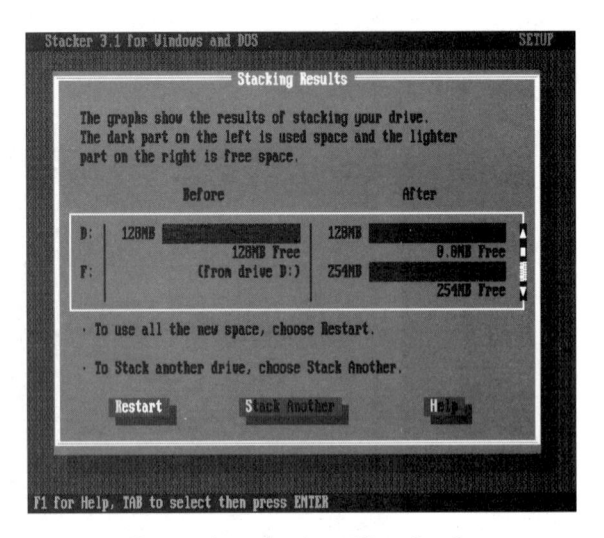

Restarting after installing Stacker

Converting a DoubleSpace drive

Stacker can also be installed by converting DoubleSpace drives to Stacker drives. Stacker removes DoubleSpace from the system and converts the compressed drive to a Stacker drive. Use the following procedure to do this:

1. Activate the Stacker installation program at the DOS prompt by typing:

    A:SETUP [Enter]

2. A welcome screen appears; choose [Continue].

3. A new screen appears, prompting you to specify your name and company. Follow the instructions. Stacker then initializes the diskettes. Make sure they are not write-protected.

4. If Stacker discovers that DoubleSpace has already been installed, it informs you of this. Stacker will convert the DoubleSpace drive to a Stacker drive.

Stacker 3.1

Chapter Five

5. Stacker recommends "C:\STACKER" as the installation directory. Confirm this by choosing [Continue].

6. Now the SETUP program begins copying the files of the compression program to the C:\STACKER directory. Depending on the system, copying the files can take from one to several minutes. During installation, the program prompts you to change diskettes. Each time you change diskettes, activate [Continue].

7. Stacker prompts you to remove the second diskette from drive A: and press [Continue]. This takes a few minutes.

8. Now Stacker begins converting the DoubleSpace drive. There are four steps to this process, which you start by choosing [Convert]. These steps are:

    - Restart the computer

    - Security check of the hard drive

    - Conversion of DoubleSpace drive to a Stacker drive

    - Restart the computer

9. Now your computer is ready to run. Your DoubleSpace drive is now a Stacker drive.

Installing Stacker for Windows

Since Stacker includes several Windows utilities, you must install them. Fortunately, you don't have to create the program group and icons manually. Instead, you can use a utility program.

Choose **Run...** from the **File** menu of the Windows Program Manager and then enter:

```
C:\STACKER\SGROUP.EXE
```

If necessary, use C:\DOS instead of C:\STACKER if you installed Stacker in the DOS directory, as we recommended. Confirm your entry by pressing [Enter]. SGroup automatically sets up a Stacker program group with all the program icons.

Chapter Five

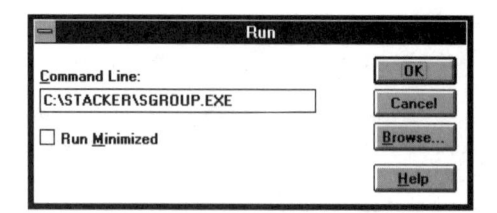

Installing Windows files for Stacker

Using Compressed Drives

Using a compressed drive is easier than you might think. Stacker ensures that the compressed drive acts like an ordinary drive on file managers, such as the DOS Shell, PC Tools, or Norton Commander, on interfaces, such as Windows and Geoworks Ensemble, as well as on application programs and DOS itself.

For example, if you want to save a file from your word processor to the compressed drive, the compressed drive appears as a normal drive entry in the "Drives" list box of the "Save As" dialog box. For example, it will appear as D: or E:. The conventional filenames and extensions apply here.

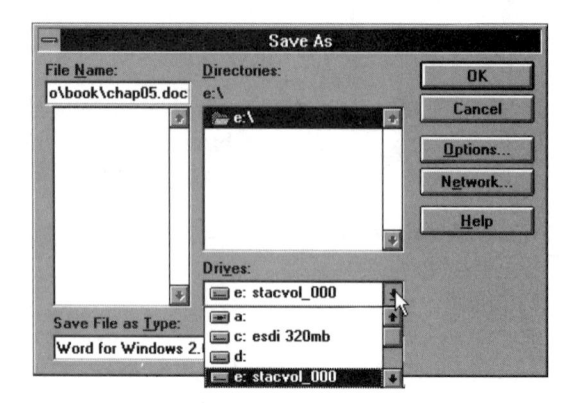

Saving a file to a compressed drive

Stacker 3.1

Chapter Five

Opening compressed files is as easy. They appear as normal files in the "File Name:" list box of the "Open" dialog box.

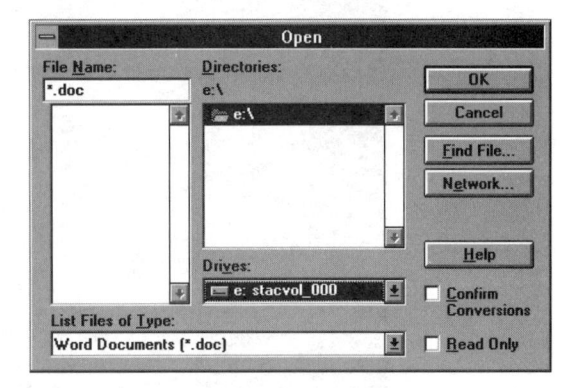

Opening a compressed file

When you open or save a file, Stacker works in the background, invisibly decompressing or compressing the data. This applies for both DOS programs and Windows applications.

MS-DOS

In DOS, you can address Stacker drives like normal hard drives and diskettes. For example, if your compressed drive is D:, then you can change to this drive by entering:

D: [Enter]

Enter the following command to display the contents of the drive:

DIR [Enter]

Chapter Five

Displaying the contents of the drive

Aside from the fact that compressed drives are named "STACVOL_xxx" by default, nothing indicates that the data is compressed. You can even change the name of the drive using the DOS Label command.

To move files from uncompressed drives to your compressed drive, enter:

```
MOVE C:DATA D: Enter
```

To set up a directory on your compressed hard drive, use the MD command:

```
MD DIRECTORY Enter
```

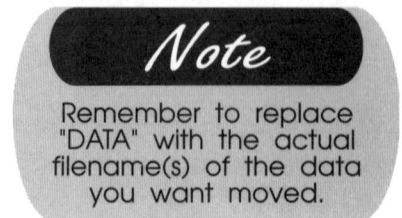

Note
Remember to replace "DATA" with the actual filename(s) of the data you want moved.

To change directories on your compressed hard drive, use the CD command:

```
CD DIRECTORY Enter
```

If you saved files on the compressed hard drive, a special option of DIR will help you determine the degree of compression. Enter the following

```
DIR /C Enter
```

Stacker 3.1

Chapter Five

to have DOS display the degree of compression for each file and the average compression ratio.

Calling DIR /C

You must use Stacker for any additional management of your compressed drive. For more information, refer to the "Managing Compressed Drives" section in this chapter.

MS-Windows

It's even easy to manage compressed drives in Windows. Activate the File Manager by double-clicking the appropriate icon in the Program Manager.

> **Note**
> Don't delete or rename any files beginning with "STAC...". These are system, initialization, and configuration files of Stacker and of the compressed hard drive. To prevent data loss, handle these files carefully.

In the drive icon bar, you'll immediately see the compressed drive highlighted as a new hard drive.

Chapter Five

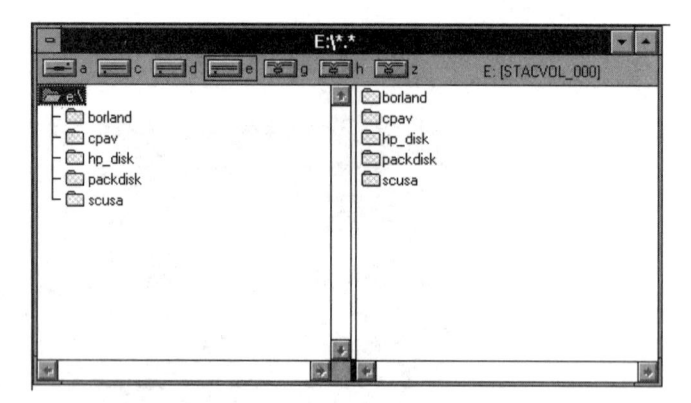

File Manager

Click on the new drive icon to change to the compressed hard drive. The File Manager also displays the name of the compressed drive as "COMPRESSED."

Select the **Create Directory...** command in the **File** menu to create new directories. Double-click the directory icons to change between directories of the compressed drive.

Use the **Copy** and **Move** commands in the **File** menu to place files on the compressed hard drive and remove them. The same commands, such as **Delete** and **Rename**, that are available for an uncompressed drive are also available for your compressed drive. Also, information about the files will be correct.

Use Stacker for any additional management of your compressed drive. Use the Stackometer program in the Stacker program group in Program Manager. For more information, refer to the "Managing Compressed Drives" section in this chapter.

> *Note*
> Don't delete or rename any files beginning with "STAC...". These are system, initialization, and configuration files of Stacker and of the compressed hard drive. To prevent data loss, handle these files carefully.

Stacker 3.1

Chapter Five

Managing Compressed Drives

The Stacker program is responsible for managing compressed drives. This involves defragmenting, verifying, enlarging, and reducing drives as well as deleting them. Remember, this isn't the same Stacker program you learned about when you installed your first compressed drive. That was the Stacker Setup program. There is a Stacker program for DOS and one for Windows.

Stacker for DOS

Never use Stacker from Windows, the DOS Shell, or any other DOS interface. Instead, always call Stacker from the DOS prompt. Stacker has a menu-driven interface which we'll describe in this chapter.

Start Stacker by entering:

```
stac Enter
```

The welcome screen, the Stacker Toolbox, appears:

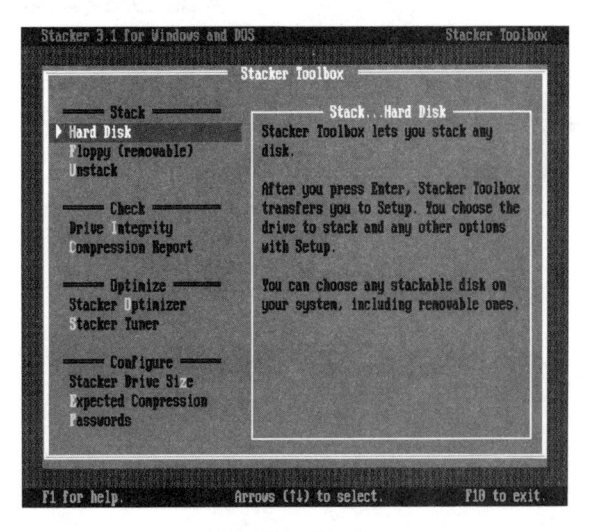

Starting Stacker

Chapter Five

Stacker interface

Although the Stacker program interface doesn't comply with the SAA/CUA standard, it's still easy to operate. To the left, you'll see a menu bar with the following groups (menus) and tools (commands):

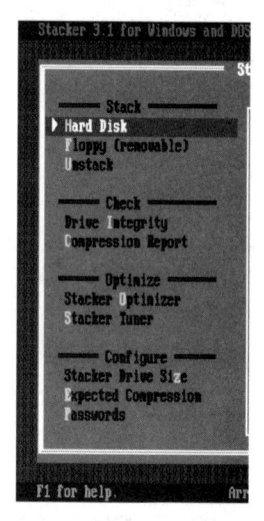

Use the cursor keys to select a group, press [Enter], and then change to the appropriate tool. For example, to obtain a compression report, select **Compression Report** from the **Check** group.

Stacker 3.1

Chapter Five

Compression Report

Use the cursor keys or the highlighted letter to activate commands. For example, you can change the sort order of the files (Show Files) or switch to Show Summary.

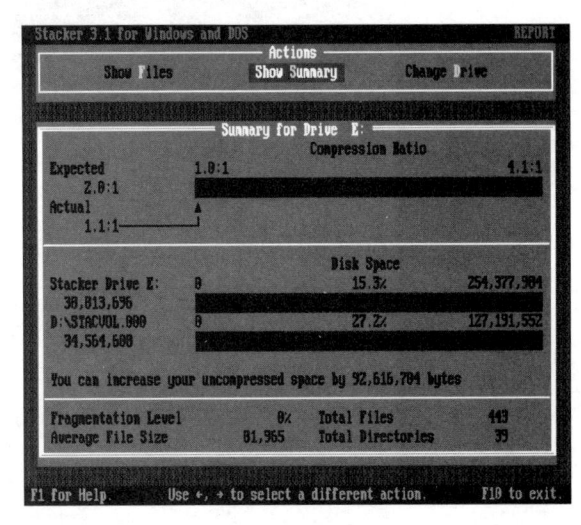

Show Summary

Chapter Five

Unfortunately, how each of these subprograms works does vary slightly, the letter you press to select a command is highlighted and the status line at the bottom displays the function keys for different actions. For example, pressing [Esc] usually ends a function.

Press [F1] to access help and then use the cursor keys to browse through the help text.

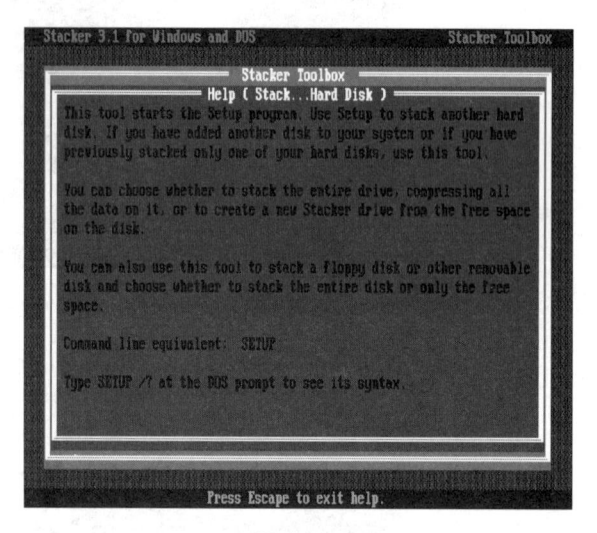

Help text

Now that you know the basics of running Stacker, we'll discuss the different functions you can use to manage Stacker.

Changing the drive size

It's possible to increase or decrease the size of your compressed hard drive. However, to increase the hard drive, the host drive must have enough free memory.

Choose the **Stacker Drive Size** command from **Configure**. The following screen appears:

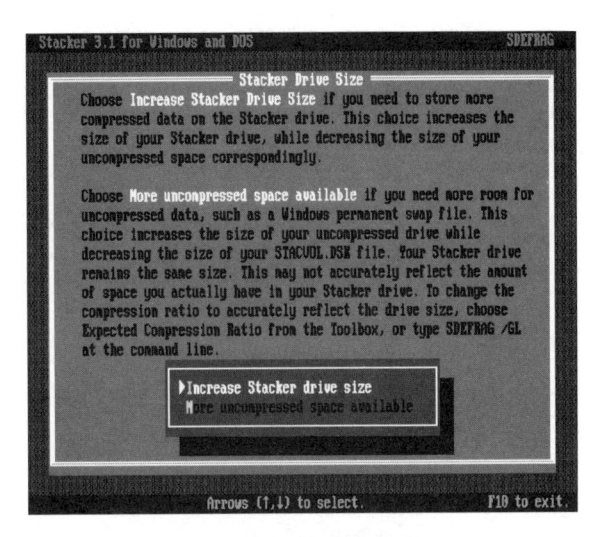

Stacker 3.1

Chapter Five

Changing the drive size

To increase the compressed drive, select the **Increase Stacker drive size** command. The other command reduces the compressed drive.

Stacker now activates SDefrag, which is a utility program that defragments the compressed hard drive. This is important because the best compression is possible only on compressed drives that aren't fragmented. Select "Yes" to have SDefrag analyze and defragment the drive. For more information about SDefrag, refer to the chapter on optimization.

Chapter Five

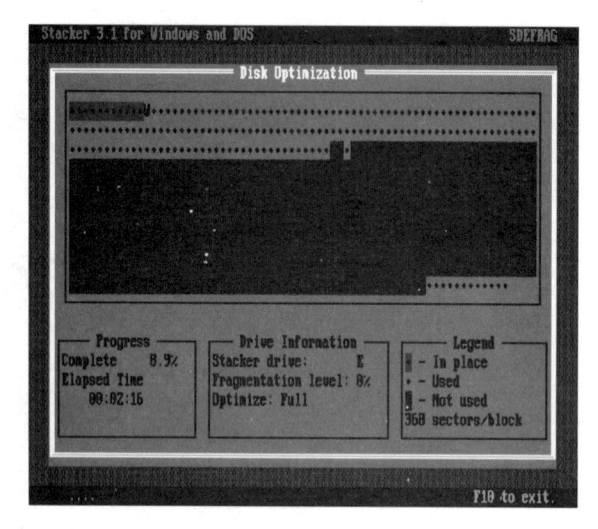

The SDEFRAG program

After defragmentation is complete, press any key to restart your computer and run Stac again. Now the "Increase Stacker Drive Size" screen appears.

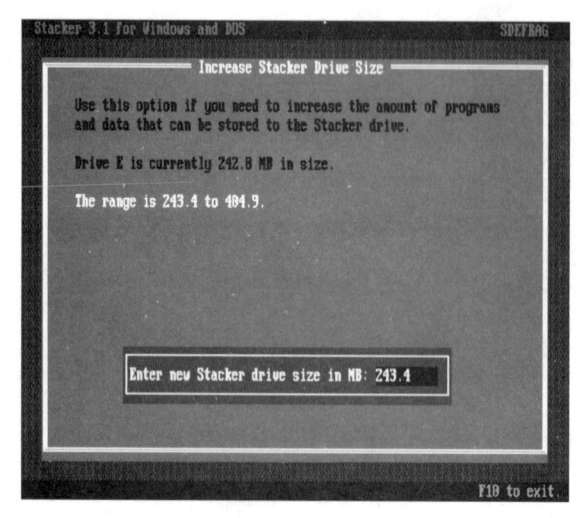

Changing the drive size

Stacker 3.1

Chapter Five

The screen displays the current size of the compressed drive and shows possible changes you can make to the drive size. Specify the desired drive size and confirm by pressing [Enter]. Then a small selection box appears at the bottom of the screen. Select **Perform changes on Stacker drive** to make the desired changes. "Modify settings" gives you another chance to think over the changes and specify a different size. Select **Exit without changes** to cancel without making any changes.

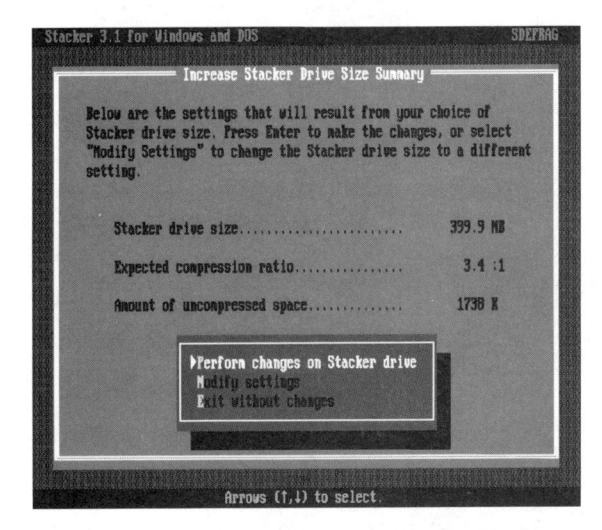

The Increase Stacker Drive Size Summary

Now Stacker begins increasing the size of the drive. Then SDefrag becomes active again, starting up Norton's Speed Disk. This program creates the necessary free space on the host drive and also defragments it.

Finally, Stacker reappears on the screen with the message "Operation Complete". Press [Enter] to restart the system. The compressed drive is now the desired size.

Chapter Five

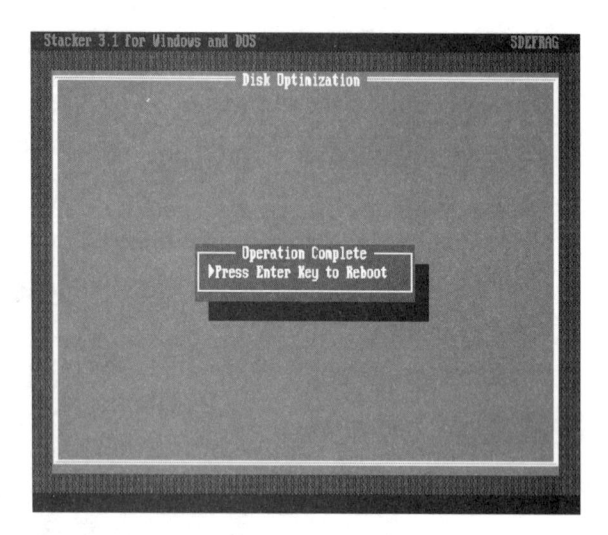

The Disk Optimization Complete message

Changing the compression ratio

As you know, the specification about the free memory on a compressed drive is an estimate based on the expected compression ratio. The default compression ratio is 2 to 1, so the size of a 50 Meg compressed hard drive is estimated to be 100 Meg. The actual size of the compressed hard drive mainly depends on the data stored on this drive and the actual compression ratio.

Stacker gives you the option of changing the compression ratio. This doesn't mean you're changing the method of compression, which would result in a greater data compression. Instead, you only change the value of the compression ratio for the estimate of free memory. For example, if you change the expected compression ratio to 3 to 1, the 50 Meg hard drive increases to an estimated 150 Meg after compression. However, if you only attain the average compression ratio of 2 to 1, the hard drive will still hold only 100 Meg of data.

As you can see, it isn't possible to make drastic changes by modifying the compression ratio. However, selecting **Expected Compression** is helpful.

Stacker 3.1

Chapter Five

When you activate **Expected Compression**, SDefrag defragments the drive first, since it's only possible to get a good estimate of the actual compression ratio on a defragmented compressed drive. When SDefrag finishes, the "Change Expected Compression Ratio" screen appears.

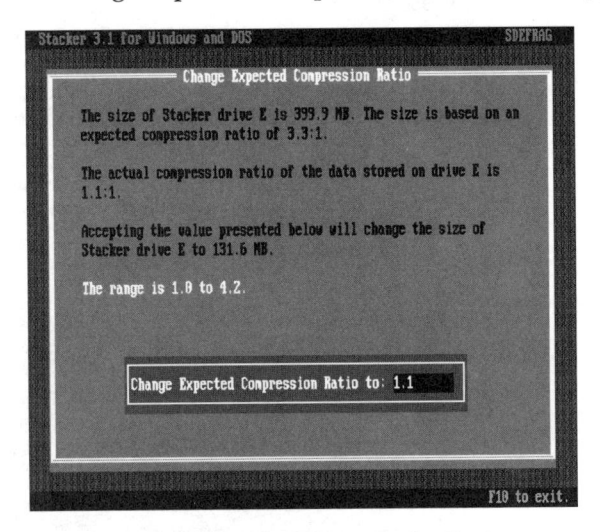

Change Expected Compression Ratio

This screen informs you of the current expected compression ratio. Specify a new ratio between 1 and 4.2.

Reduce the expected ratio if you plan to save only files that don't compress well. Increase the ratio if you want to place data that compresses well, such as texts, tables, databases, and graphics, on your compressed hard drive. For information on how well specific file types compress, refer to the "Compression Ratios" section in Chapter 2.

Confirm your changes by pressing [Enter] and select **Perform Changes on Stacker drive**. The "Operation Complete" message will appear. Press [Enter] to confirm this message. Stacker then restarts your computer.

Chapter Five

Defragmenting drives

Even compressed drives can become fragmented, so occasionally you must defragment, or optimize, your compressed drive. However, you cannot use the DOS utility, DEFRAG, to do this. Instead you must call a special Stacker command. Activate **Stacker Optimizer**.

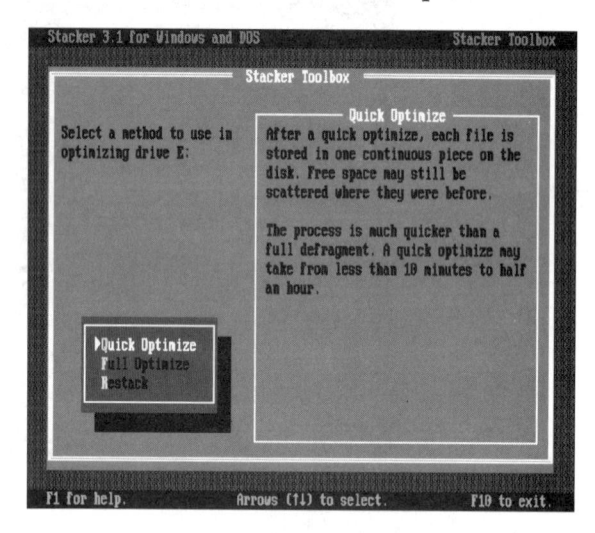

Optimization methods

Quick Optimize is a quick method of optimization. Fragmented files are defragmented, but free memory remains scattered. **Full Optimize** also defragments files and free memory. **Restack** performs full optimization and then recompresses all the files. This takes quite a while, but results in a significant gain in memory. Generally, **Quick Optimize** is suitable.

Now Stacker checks the file allocation tables and directory information. Then it analyzes the fragmentation and displays the information on the screen. Starting at 10% fragmentation, you should defragment. To do this, click Continue. Otherwise, activate **Exit SDefrag**.

Stacker 3.1

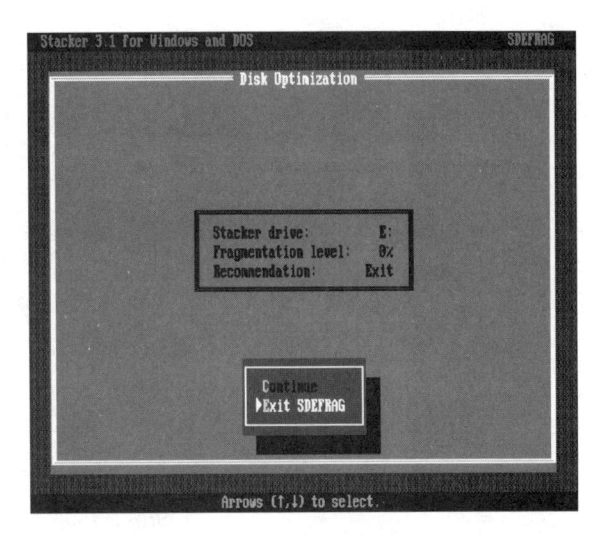

Chapter Five

Fragmentation

After you press Continue, Stacker rewrites the directories, rearranges the files, and checks the clusters.

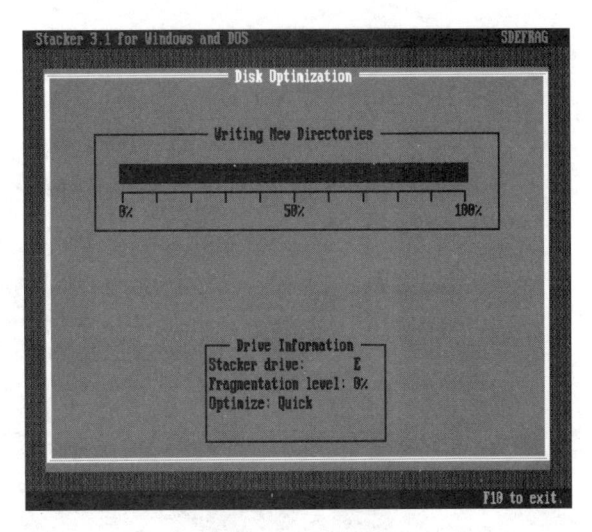

Running SDefrag

When Stacker is finished, the "Optimization Complete" message appears. Press Enter to confirm this message.

Stacker 3.1

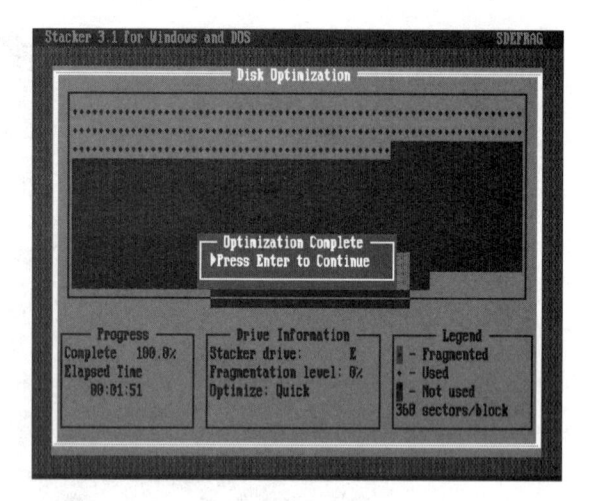

Chapter Five

Optimization

Then you'll return to the Stacker Toolbox.

Checking the drive

Even a compressed drive must be checked sometimes. To check the internal structure of the STACVOL file, select **Drive Integrity** from the **Stacker** menu.

Checking directories and files

Stacker 3.1

Chapter Five

Stacker switches to DOS and checks the structure of the directories and files. If nothing is wrong with the structure, Stacker displays the message, "Do you wish to perform a disk surface test?". This means that you have the option of running a surface test of the disk. Confirm this prompt by typing Y and pressing Enter.

Confirming a disk surface test

Stacker reads and scans all the clusters of the compressed drive. Then it displays a message about the achieved compression and expected free disk space on the compressed drive. Press any key to continue. You then return to the Stacker Toolbox.

Press F10 to exit the program. Confirm the security prompt with "Yes."

Stacker for Windows

There is also a Windows version of Stacker.

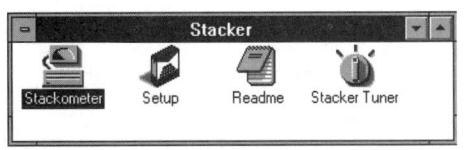

The Stacker Group

To run Stacker in Windows, click on the Stackometer icon in the Stacker program group. The following screen appears:

Chapter Five

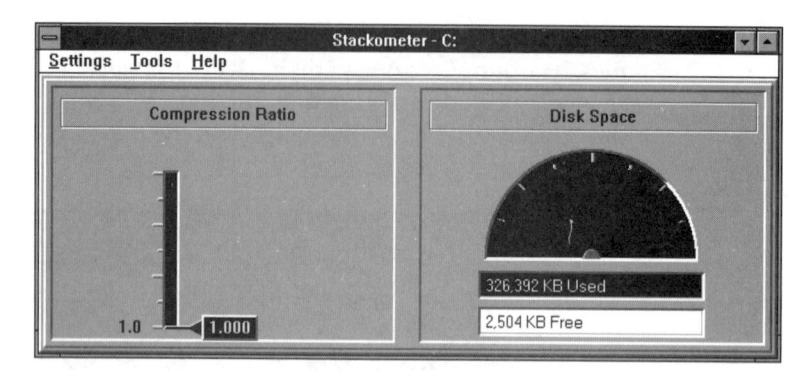

Starting Stackometer

First, select the compressed drive, since the Stackometer doesn't know which drive is compressed. Then activate **Select Drive** from the **Settings** menu.

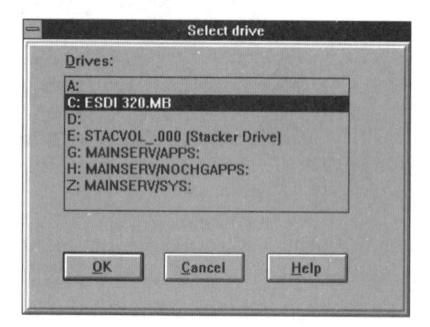

Selecting a drive

Select the compressed drive and click OK. The Stackometer displays the compression ratio, the amount of used and free disk space on the compressed drive, and the fragmentation level.

Stacker 3.1

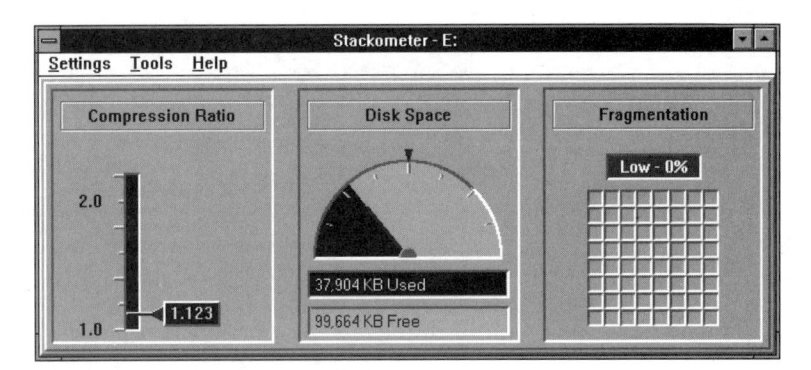

Chapter Five

Drive analysis

Changing the compression ratio

As you know, the specification about the free memory on a compressed drive is an estimate based on the expected compression ratio. The default compression ratio is 2 to 1, so the size of a 50 Meg compressed hard drive is estimated to be 100 Meg. The actual size of the compressed hard drive mainly depends on the data stored on this drive and the actual compression ratio.

Stacker gives you the option of changing the compression ratio. This doesn't mean you're changing the method of compression, which would result in a greater data compression. Instead, you change only the value of the compression ratio for the estimate of free memory. For example, if you change the expected compression ratio to 3 to 1, the 50 Meg hard drive increases to an estimated 150 Meg after compression. However, the hard drive will still hold only 100 Meg of data if only the average compression ratio of 2 to 1 is attained.

As you can see, it isn't possible to make drastic changes by modifying the compression ratio. However, activating **Set Expected Compression** in the **Tools** menu is helpful.

Chapter Five

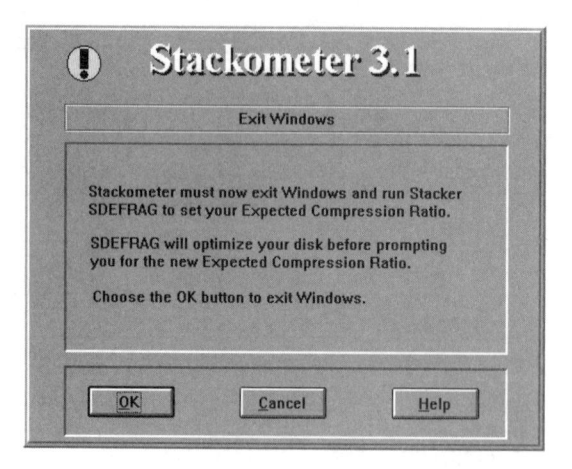

Exiting Windows

When you activate **Expected Compression**, SDefrag defragments the drive first, since it's only possible to get a good estimate of the actual compression ratio on a defragmented compressed drive. To do this, Stacker must exit Windows. Click OK to exit Windows. When SDefrag is finished, the "Change Expected Compression Ratio" screen appears:

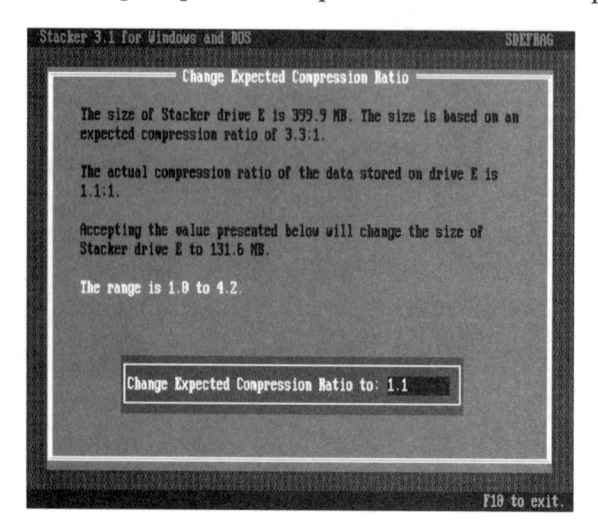

Change Expected Compression Ratio

Stacker 3.1

Chapter Five

This screen informs you of the current expected compression ratio. Specify a new ratio between 1 and 4.2.

Reduce the expected ratio if you plan to save only files that don't compress well. Increase the ratio if you want to place data that compresses well, such as texts, tables, databases, and graphics, on your compressed hard drive. For information on how well specific file types compress, refer to the "Compression Ratios" section in Chapter 2.

Confirm your changes by pressing [Enter] and selecting **Perform Changes on Stacker drive**. The "Operation Complete" message will appear. Press [Enter] to confirm this message. Stacker then restarts your computer and you must activate Windows again.

Defragmenting files

Because even compressed drives can become fragmented, you must occasionally defragment, or optimize, your compressed drive. However, you cannot use the DOS utility DEFRAG to do this. Instead, you must call a special Stacker command.

In the **Tools** menu, select one of the following commands:

Quick Optimize

This command is a quick method of optimization. Fragmented files are defragmented, but free memory remains scattered. Generally, **Quick Optimize** is acceptable.

Note: Again, Stacker must exit Windows.

Full Optimize

This command also defragments free memory.

Restack

This command performs full optimization and then recompresses all the files. This takes quite a while, but results in a significant gain in memory.

Stacker 3.1

Chapter Five

Now Stacker checks the file allocation tables and directory information. Then it analyzes the fragmentation and displays the information on the screen. Starting at 10% fragmentation, you should defragment. To do this, click [Continue]. Otherwise, select **Exit SDefrag**.

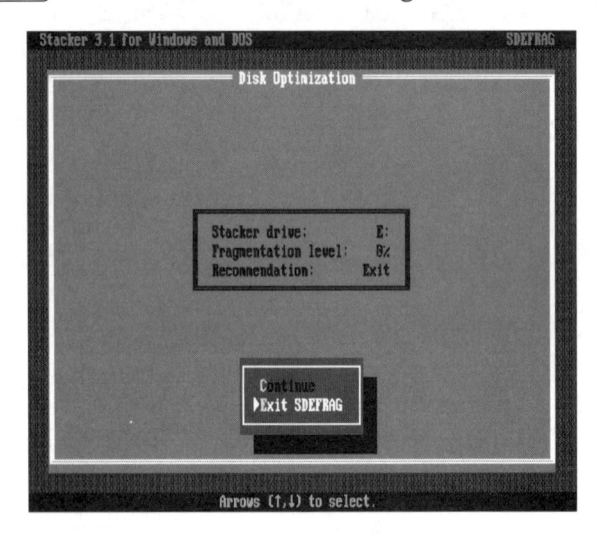

Fragmentation

After you press [Continue], Stacker rewrites the directories, rearranges the files, and checks the clusters. When Stacker is finished, the "Optimization Complete" message appears. Press [Enter] to confirm this message.

Stacker 3.1

Chapter Five

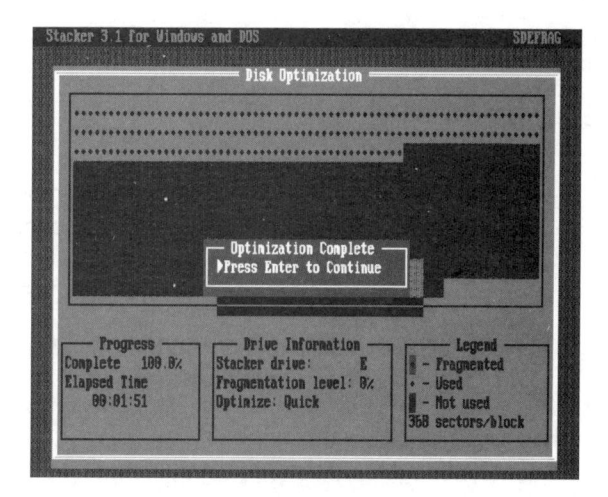

Optimization

Then you return to DOS.

Optimizing the Hard Drive

Ever since PCs first appeared, optimization has been important. The main purpose of optimizing, or improving the performance of your PC, is increasing the processing speed. When you use Stacker, the size of the available hard drive disk space, the use of RAM, and access speed are important.

More space for the hard drive

Installing Stacker and compressed drives on your system is a major part of optimizing the free disk space on your hard drive. Once you've done that, there's not much more you can do.

If you compressed only part of your hard drive, you can change the size of the compressed hard drive, thus increasing the amount of available disk space. For information on how to do this, refer to the "Stacker for Windows" information beginning on page 169.

Chapter Five

Delete files that you don't need. Even a compressed hard drive can quickly collect unnecessary data garbage such as .TMP files, .BAK files, etc. To determine what you can delete, refer to the "Deleting unnecessary files" information beginning on page 137.

The amount of free disk space you specify on a compressed STACVOL file (STACKER drive) depends mainly on the expected compression ratio. The expected compression ratio starts as 2 to 1; later the ratio depends on the actual compression ratio for the files currently stored on the drive.

However, if you know that the files you'll be saving in the future will produce a much better compression ratio, you should increase the expected compression ratio. This simultaneously increases the amount of free disk space that's available. However, be sure that the files you plan on saving really do meet your expectations.

Refer to the "Managing Compressed Drives" section in this chapter to learn about this procedure. For more information on achievable compression ratios, see the "Compression Ratios" section in Chapter 2.

Finally, you can increase the amount of free disk space on your hard drive by better use of the compressed hard drive. This is especially helpful when your compression ratio has been below 2 to 1 and you still have many files stored on your uncompressed drive that compress well. Move files that compress well to the compressed drive and move files that compress poorly from the compressed drive to the uncompressed drive.

More free RAM

If it seems like the amount of disk space for DOS or Windows has decreased since you started using Stacker, or that there isn't enough disk space to run an application that ran before you installed Stacker, you must optimize RAM and its usage. To do this, use MEMMAKER, which we discussed in detail in Chapter 3.

You should also remove necessary drivers and other memory-resident programs. If you don't know whether these drivers and programs are necessary, use the REM command in the CONFIG.SYS and AUTOEXEC.BAT files to temporarily disable drivers and programs. Remember that you need STAC.SYS or STACHIGH.SYS because these drivers load the Stacker system.

Stacker 3.1

Chapter Five

Memory-resident virus monitors, delete-protection programs, and desktop programs, such as Sidekick or PC Desktop from PC Tools, aren't necessary to your system. The DOS drivers GRAFTABL and GRAPHICS don't have to be installed either. After permanently removing unnecessary drivers and programs, run MEMMAKER again.

Higher access speed

Obviously you want to guarantee the highest possible access speed for reading data from or writing data to your compressed hard drive. However, there are limits to what you can do. If your computer is slow and the hard drive isn't very fast, you won't be able to make your PC extremely fast by using DoubleSpace.

However, by using the following tips, you can increase the access speed:

- Defragment the compressed hard drive regularly. For more information, see the "Managing Compressed Drives" section in this chapter.

- Check the structure of the compressed hard drive often. For more information, see the "Managing Compressed Drives" section.

- Delete unnecessary files. Even a compressed hard drive can quickly collect unnecessary data garbage, such as .TMP files, .BAK files, etc. To determine what you can delete, refer to the "Deleting unnecessary files" information starting on page 137.

- If you have large files that compress well and it takes too much time to open and save them, it may be better to have smaller files that don't compress as well. The less you have to compress, the faster you can load and save. However, by doing this, you're wasting disk space.

Stacker Tuner

Stacker has an optimization program for DOS and Windows called Stacker Tuner. In Windows, you can activate the Tuner by clicking on the appropriate icon in the Stacker program group. In DOS, activate the Tuner by entering:

```
tuner Enter
```

Chapter Five

The following screens appear; both have the same function.

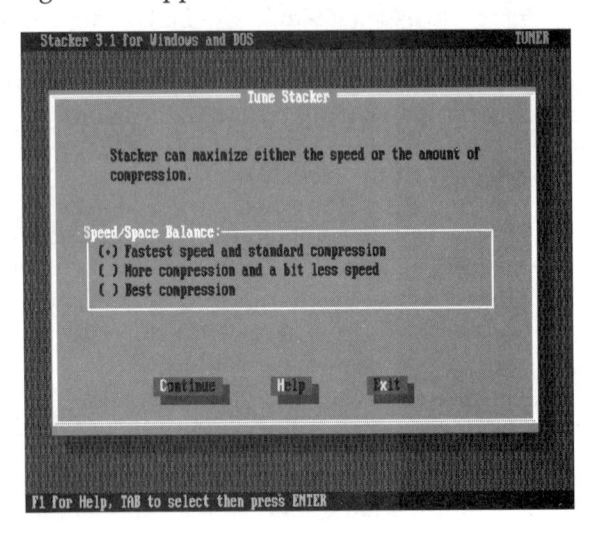

DOS-Tuner

You can also access the DOS-Tuner by selecting **Stacker Tuner** from the Stacker Program Group.

Windows-Tuner

Stacker 3.1

Chapter Five

You can choose from different operating modes for Stacker. These are the same choices that were available when you installed Stacker. However, perhaps your needs have changed since then.

Fastest speed and standard compression

This mode provides normal compression and high working speed.

More compression and a bit less speed

This mode increases the compression ratio while maintaining a high speed in accessing the compressed data.

Best compression

This mode emphasizes compression over speed.

Choose the appropriate mode and click [Continue] or [OK]. The Stacker INI file is changed, and you're prompted to confirm the changes by clicking [OK]. These new settings won't become effective until you reboot the system.

Stacker and Other Applications

Stacker is usually compatible with your applications. However, occasionally you must create compatibility by using a trick or some special precautions. We'll discuss these special cases in this section.

Cache programs

Not all cache programs are compatible with Stacker. For example, Stacker Setup may indicate that your computer is running an incompatible cache program. Do the following to avoid this error message:

1. Open your CONFIG.SYS and AUTOEXEC.BAT system files and delete the line containing the command that loads your disk caching program.

2. Save the file and reboot your computer by pressing [Ctrl] + [Alt] + [Del].

Chapter Five

Windows swap file

For technical reasons, the Windows permanent swap file cannot be on a compressed drive. However, the Windows Control Panel does allow you to create the swap file on a compressed drive, even if this is not a good idea. When you install Stacker, the swap file is automatically moved to the uncompressed part of the hard drive.

If your permanent Windows swap file is on a compressed drive, Windows displays the message "The permanent swap file is corrupt" at startup. Follow these steps to solve this problem:

1. Start Windows.

2. In the "Permanent Swap File damaged" dialog box, answer the question "Do you want to delete this swap file?" by typing [Y] and press [Enter].

3. After starting Windows, open the Control Panel and double-click the 386 Enhanced icon.

4. Click the [Virtual Memory] button. Windows displays a dialog box indicating that a damaged swap file has been found and asks whether you want to set the file length to zero.

5. Click [Yes]. Windows displays another dialog box, called "Virtual Memory."

6. Click the [Change] button. Windows displays the settings of the swap file.

Note
If your uncompressed drive doesn't have enough free memory to create a permanent swap file, create a temporary swap file on your compressed or uncompressed drives.

7. In the "Drive" list box, choose a drive that isn't compressed. In the "Type" list box, choose "Permanent."

8. After you've made the settings, click [OK] twice. Windows displays a dialog box that prompts you to restart Windows.

9. Click the [Restart Windows] button.

Stacker 3.1

Chapter Five

Compressed files

Some files (for example, .ZIP, .ARC, .LZH files) are already compressed. Stacker may not be able to compress these files again.

Encrypted data files, such as .MMF files of Microsoft Mail 3.0, cannot be compressed either. These files are saved in uncompressed form, even if you store them on a compressed drive.

It's better to store uncompressed files on a drive that isn't compressed. This can increase the speed of your system.

DOS DEFRAG

Calling the DOS 6 defragmentation program doesn't activate Norton Defrag on drives compressed by Stacker. Instead, it calls the Stacker SDefrag program. However, you can use SDefrag to defragment compressed drives similar to the way Norton's Defrag defragments normal drives.

Common Error Messages

Although you may encounter problems while using Stacker, often these problems are easily solved. In this section, we'll discuss some common error messages and show you how to eliminate them.

The compressed drive does not have enough disk space

If your compressed drive no longer has enough disk space, you can use one of the following methods to make more disk space available:

- Increase the size of the drive (see the "Managing Compressed Drives" section in this chapter).

- Specify a higher expected compression ratio for the drive (see the "Managing Compressed Drives" section in this chapter).

Chapter Five

- Use SDefrag, the optimization commands of the Stacker Toolbox, or the Stackometer to defragment the compressed drive.

The uncompressed drive does not have enough disk space

If your uncompressed drive (host drive) no longer has enough disk space, you can increase its size by reducing the size of the compressed drive(s) stored on the uncompressed drive. Naturally, this also reduces the amount of free memory on the compressed drive(s). Refer to the "Managing Compressed Drives" section in this chapter for more information.

Stacker doesn't compress all the files, because enough disk space isn't available

If Stacker indicates that it couldn't compress some of your files because there isn't enough available disk space, do the following:

1. Back up the files that are still uncompressed on the host drive, to diskettes.
2. Now delete those uncompressed files from the host drive.
3. Enter "STAC" at the DOS prompt.
4. Now select **Change Drive Size** from the menu and increase the compressed drive to full size.
5. Copy the backed up files back to your host drive.

Stacker reports a damaged CVF

If the message, "CVF is damaged", appears on your screen after you start your computer, this means that Stacker found a problem with the compressed STACVOL file. This usually occurs when there are cross-linked files on the compressed drive. Stacker detects a cross-linked file when two files or directories are entered in the Stacker File Allocation Table as using the same disk space.

You can eliminate this problem by checking the compressed hard drive. For information on how to do this, refer to the "Managing Compressed Drives" section in this chapter.

Stacker 3.1

Chapter Five

Removing Stacker

Perhaps you're wondering why we would discuss uninstalling Stacker's compression software in a book that discusses the advantages of data compression. However, eventually you may want to do this for some reason.

There is no method for automatically removing Stacker. Instead, you must remove it manually, by following these steps:

1. Back up the files on the compressed drive. If you use a backup program, its program files must be on a different drive or on a diskette.

2. Determine on which uncompressed drive the compressed drive is stored. For example, you could use the DOS Shell. Search for the STACVOL.00? file, replacing the ? with a number.

3. Copy the COMMAND.COM file from the compressed drive to the root directory of your uncompressed drive, if necessary.

4. To delete your Stacker files, make your uncompressed drive the current drive. Now enter the following at the DOS prompt:

   ```
   cd \STACKER Enter
   ERASE *.* Enter
   ```

   Also delete the compressed STACVOL file in the root directory.

5. Open the CONFIG.SYS file in the DOS Editor and remove the Stacker driver.

6. Restart your computer by pressing Ctrl + Alt + Del.

7. Now copy back the files you backed up. Naturally, this is only possible if there is enough room on the uncompressed hard drive for all your data.

Stacker 3.1

Chapter Five

You have now removed Stacker and at the same time, made a backup of the compressed data. You probably won't be able to copy all the data back to the hard drive. After all, the data was compressed, so it only took up half the space.

Uncompressing Drives

Stacker also gives you the option of uncompressing compressed drives. To do this, use the Stacker Toolbox. To call the Toolbox, enter the following at the DOS prompt:

STAC [Enter]

However, there is a catch. If you've filled up the entire compressed drive, it probably contains more data than will fit on the free space of the hard drive in uncompressed form. In other words, you cannot perform decompression unless you first reduce the amount of data on the compressed drive.

Select the **Unstack** command from the **Stack** menu. A dialog box appears in the lower-left corner. From the menu in this dialog box, select the drive you want to unstack (decompress).

Stacker 3.1

Chapter Five

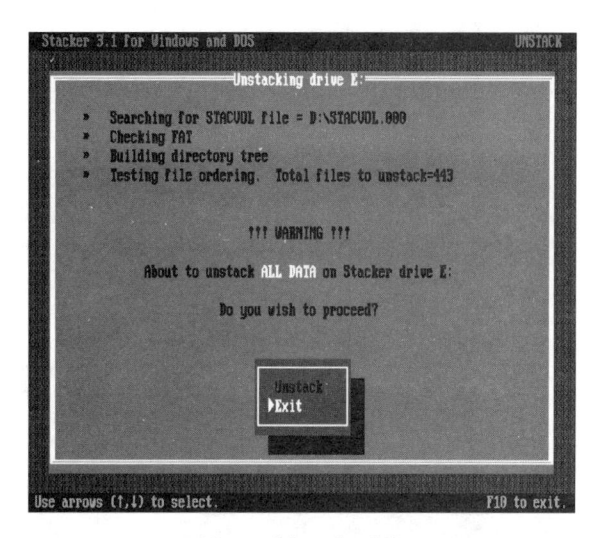

Unstacking the drive

Stacker immediately begins unstacking, or decompressing, the drive. A security prompt appears twice. Confirm these prompts by choosing "Yes -- proceed." After Stacker finishes unstacking the drive, you must press [Enter] again to exit to DOS, so you can restart the system. Only by restarting the system do you update the system environment.

Stacker Command Lines

You can also call Stacker commands from the DOS prompt. The following table is an overview of the different commands. We'll explain each command in more detail on the following pages.

Stacker 3.1

Chapter Five

Check	Checks the compressed drive
Create	Compresses floppy disks
Ed	Loads the Stacker text editor
Passwd	Protects compressed drives with a password
Preview	Determines the expected compression ratio
Removdrv	Removes a Stacker drive
Report	Outputs a compression report
SAttrib	Changes the file attributes on compressed drives
SDefrag	Defragments compressed drives
SDir	Displays the actual compression ratio
Setup	Installs Stacker or additional compressed drives
Stacker	Loads compressed diskettes
Tuner	Optimizes the compressed drives
Unstack	Decompresses a compressed drive

Check

Checks the compressed drive.

Syntax

```
check [drive:] [/B] [/F] [/D] [/V] [/?] [/WP]
```

Parameters

   drive: Specifies the name of the compressed drive.

Switches

   /B   Suppresses all pauses and prompts from Check, as long as no repairs to compressed drives are necessary.

Stacker 3.1

Chapter Five

/F	Enables Check to repair errors and, if desired, performs a surface scan.
/D	Displays additional information, such as the level of fragmentation.
/V	Lists the files and directories that have been checked.
/?	Displays the help screen.
/WP	Quickly searches for damaged Stacker drives and asks whether damages should be repaired.

Create

Compresses disk drives.

Syntax

```
create drive: [stacvol.xxx] [/S=nnn.n[K|M] [/R=n.n] [C=n] [/B] [/M] [/?]
```

Parameters

drive:	Specifies drive to be compressed.
stacvol.xxx	Specifies the name of the compressed STACVOL file. xxx can be replaced by a consecutive number or by the default, DSK.

Switches

/S=nnn.nK	Specifies the amount of disk space for compression. The nnn.n represents kilobytes, which explains the K.
/S=nnn.nM	Specifies the amount of disk space for compression. The nnn.n represent megabytes, which explains the M.

Stacker 3.1

Chapter Five

/R=n.n Specifies the size of the compressed drive by an expected compression ratio of n.n, which can range from 1.0 to 8.0. /S=20 /R=2.5 creates a compressed drive with a maximum of 50 Meg of free memory out of 20 Meg of free disk space.

/C=n Sets the cluster size on compressed drives to n=4, 8, 16 or 32. 8 is the default.

/B Suppresses all screen messages from Create.

/M Switches to monochrome display.

/? Displays the help screen.

DCONVERT

(MS-DOS 6 only) Converts a DoubleSpace compressed disk to a Stacker disk.

Syntax

```
dconvert [/m] /c <DoubleSpace Volume> | /g <DoubleSpace Volume> <Stacker Volume>
```

Switches

/M Switches to monochrome display.

/c <DoubleSpace Volume>
  Converts a DoubleSpace Volume to a Stacker Volume.

/g <DoubleSpace Volume> <Stacker Volume>
  Generates a Stacker volume from a DoubleSpace volume.

Stacker 3.1

Chapter Five

Ed

Loads the Stacker text editor, which lets you edit .INI, CONFIG.SYS, and .BAT files. Working with the text editor is like working with a word processor. Add the name of the file you want to edit to the command as a parameter; the text editor then opens the file immediately. Use the following key combinations with ED:

Ctrl S	Searches from present cursor location to the end of a document for a specifed text string.
Ctrl R	Searches from present cursor location to the beginning of a document for a specifed text string.
Alt C	Copies a selected block.
Alt E	Ends selection of a text block.
Alt S	Starts selection of a text block.
Alt X	Deletes the selected text block.
Backspace	Deletes the character to the left of the cursor.
Ctrl K	Deletes from the cursor to the end of the line.
Ctrl Q	Enters the next character as control code. For example, to produce a form feed, press Ctrl + Q + L.
Ctrl Y	Pastes a cut text block back in the text.
Ctrl Z	Saves the file and returns to DOS.
Del	Deletes the character at the cursor position.
Esc	Exits Ed. A security prompt to save appears.
F2	Loads a new file for editing.
F3	Saves a file under a name to be specified.
Ins	Switches between insert and overtype modes.

Chapter Five

Ed Text editor

Passwd

Protects compressed drives with a password.

Syntax

```
passwd drive: [.|oldpassword] [newpassword|.] [/RO]
```

Parameters

drive:	Specifies the drive to be protected by a password.
.	Used to indicate that no old password exists.
oldpassword	Specifies the old password.
newpassword	Specifies the new password.
.	Specifies that there will be no new password. In other words, this parameter cancels password protection.

Stacker 3.1

Chapter Five

Switches

/RO   Assigns passwords that only apply to read operations (Read Only).

Preview

Determines the expected compression ratio for a drive that is not compressed.

Syntax

```
preview [drive:] [/M]
```

Parameters

drive: Specifies the drive to be previewed. If you don't specify a parameter, PREVIEW opens a dialog box and prompts you to select a drive. The current drive is selected as the default drive.

Switches

/M   Switches to monochrome display.

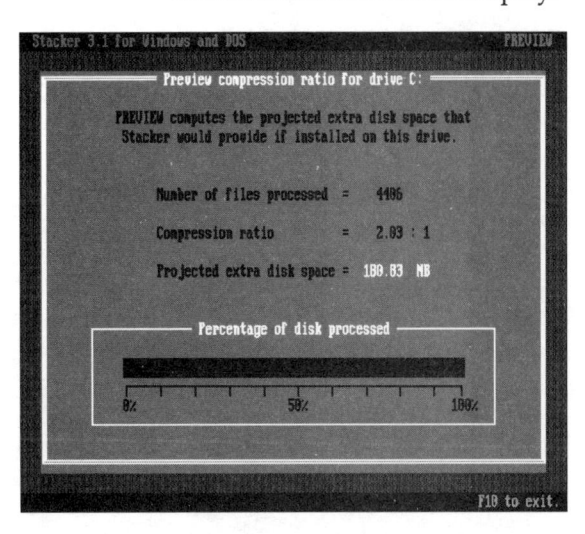

Compression prediction

Chapter Five

Removdrv

Removes a Stacker drive. In the process, all data on the compressed drive is deleted.

Syntax

```
removdrv drive: [/M]
```

Parameters

  drive: Names the drive to be removed.

Switches

  /M   Switches to monochrome display.

Report

Outputs a compression report.

Syntax

```
report [/M]
```

Switches

  /M   Switches to monochrome display.

Stacker 3.1

Chapter Five

Compression report

SAttrib

Changes the file attributes of files on compressed drives. SAttrib is completely compatible with the DOS Attrib command.

Use SAttrib to set and clear file attributes. For example, you can hide documents you want kept secret, make important documents into system files, or make templates Read Only.

Syntax

```
SATTRIB [options] filename.ext[[ filename.ext][ filename.ext]...]
```

Switches

-	Turns off the selected attribute.
+	Turns on the selected attribute.
A	Archive attribute.
H	Hidden attribute.

Chapter Five

R	Read-only attribute.
S	System attribute.
filename.ext	The filespec to which the attribute changes apply.
/?	Displays the help screen.

Example

`attrib Filename`

Displays Read-Only and Archive attributes of files

`attrib +r Filename`

Sets the Read-Only attribute

`attrib -r Filename`

Clears the Read-Only attribute

`attrib +a Filename`

Sets the Archive attribute

`attrib -a Filename`

Clears the Archive attribute

SDefrag

Defragments a compressed drive.

Syntax

```
sdefrag [drive:] [/R] [/GL] [/GP] [/D] [/F] [/Sx] [/P=#] [U] [/B] [/BATCH] [/SKIPHIGH] [/LCD] [/BW] [/H] [/V] / RESTORE=x:STACVOL.ext
```

Parameters

   drive: Specifies the drive to be decompressed.

Stacker 3.1

Chapter Five

Switches

/R	Recompress data to minimize space
/GL	Change expected compression ratio for Stacker drive
/GP	Increase size of Stacker drive or creates more uncompressed space
/D	Optimize directory only
/F	Full optimization
Sx	Sort file information in the following order:

        N   by file name (default)
        E   by file extension
        D   by time of creation
        S   by file size
        U   no sort
        -     following any of the above reverses the normal order

/P=#	Recompress data using level # (where # is from 1 to 9)
/U	Quick optimization
/B	Reboot computer after optimization
/BATCH	Run in batch mode
/SKIPHIGH	Skip loading data in high memory
/LCD	Use Monochrome display color set
/BW	Use Monochrome display color set
/H	Move hidden files
/V	Use write verify mode

Chapter Five

/RESTORE=x:STACVOL.ext
        Restores Stacker drive if optimization was interrupted by rebooting or a power failure

/?   Display the help screen

SDir

Displays the contents of compressed drives. To a large extent, this command is compatible with the DOS DIR command.

SDIR displays the contents of directories on the drive.

Syntax

```
dir pathname
```

Displays all appropriate files in the pathname.

Switches

/P	Pause after each page.
/W	List files in wide display.
/H	Show all hidden files.
/A	Display files with specified attributes.

        D   Directories
        R   Read-only files
        H   Hidden files
        S   System files
        A   Files ready to archive
        -     Prefix meaning "not"; displays files which don't have the specified attributes

Stacker 3.1

Chapter Five

/O		List files in specified sorted order.
	N	By name (alphabetic)
	S	By size (smallest first)
	E	By extension (alphabetic)
	D	By date & time (earliest first)
	G	Group directories first
	-	Prefix to reverse order
	C	By compression ratio (smallest first)
/S		Display files in the specified directory and all subdirectories.
/B		Use bare format (no heading information or summary).
/L		Use lowercase.
/C[H]		Displays file compression ratio; /CH uses host allocation unit size.

Setup

Installs Stacker or sets up new compressed drives.

Syntax

`setup [/AT] [/MC] [/XT] [/M]`

Switches

/M	Switches to monochrome display.
/T=<drive>	Specify a temporary installation location.
/?	Display help screen.

Note: For more information on Setup, see the "Installing Stacker" section in this chapter.

Chapter Five

> **Stacker**

Show Stacker drive map, or mount/unmount Stacker drives.

Syntax

```
STACKER [-]d1:
```

or

```
STACKER d2:=d3:\STACVOL.xxx
```

or

```
STACKER @d4:\STACVOL.xxx
```

Switches

[-]d1:   Mounts the STACVOL.DSK file on drive d1 as Stacker drive d1. Using the optional '-' unmounts Stacker drive d1.

d2:=d3:\STACVOL.xxx
           Mounts d3:\STACVOL.xxx as drive d2.

@d4:\STACVOL.xxx   Mounts d4:\STACVOL.xxx as drive d4.

/?   Displays the help screen.

If no options are given, the current Stacker drive map is displayed.

> **Tuner**

Optimizes the compressed drives. Starts the Tuner program described in the section on optimization.

Syntax

```
tuner
```

Stacker 3.1

Chapter Five

Unstack

Uncompresses a compressed drive. The procedure is described in the "Uncompressing Drives" section in this chapter.

Syntax

```
unstack [drive:] [/M]
```

Parameters

    drive: Specifies the drive to be decompressed.

Switches

    /M   Switches to monochrome display.

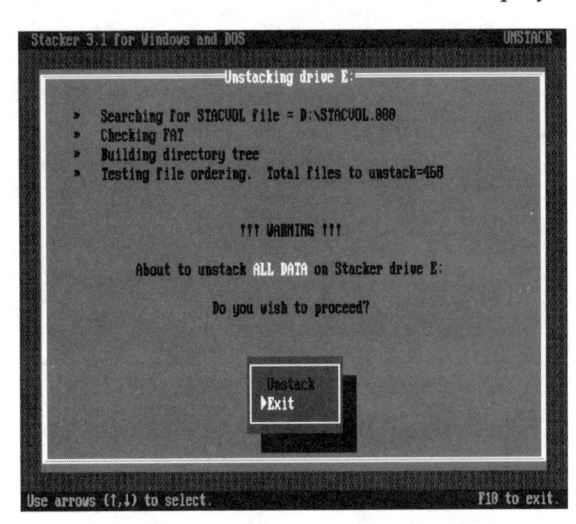

Decompression

The following overview of commands is important for users switching from DOS DoubleSpace to Stacker. It lists the names of DOS commands and the eqivalent Stacker command.

Chapter Five

DOS	Stacker
CHKDSK (and all parameters)	CHECK (and all parameters)
DBLSPACE/CHK	CHECK
DBLSPACE/DEF	SDEFRAG
DBLSPACE/LIST	STACKER
DBLSPACE/MO drive:	STACKER drive:
DBLSPACE/U drive:	STACKER -drive:
DIR/C	SDIR
DIR/C/P	SDIR/P
DIR/C/H	SDIR/H
DIR/C/W	SDIR/W
DEFRAG	SDEFRAG
DEFRAG/F	SDEFRAG
DEFRAG/U	SDEFRAG/Q
DEFRAG/B	SDEFRAG
DEFRAG/SN	SDEFRAG/SN
DEFRAG/SE	SDEFRAG/SE
DEFRAG/SD	SDEFRAG/SD
DEFRAG/SS	SDEFRAG/SS
DEFRAG/LCD	SDEFRAG/M
DEFRAG/BW	SDEFRAG/M
DEFRAG/CO	SDEFRAG
DEFRAG/SKIPHIGH	SDEFRAG

Stacker 3.1

Chapter Five

DOS	Stacker
FORMAT/S	Copies DBLSPACE.BIN, which has been modified by Stacker, to the formatted diskette during formatting.
SYS	Copies DBLSPACE.BIN, which has been modified by Stacker, to the formatted diskette.

However, you can also change all the settings in STACKER.INI from the Stacker Toolbox and the Setup program.

Also, the FILELIST.TXT file contains a listing of which files are important for Stacker and the significance of each file.

Note

You may also want to change the STACKER.INI file. This file is hidden in the Stacker directory. To find out, read the README.TXT file, which you can view with Ed.

Chapter 6

Inside DoubleSpace

Contents

Command Lines 205

Extensions in DOS 6.2 214

The DoubleSpace API 217

Inside DoubleSpace

Chapter Six

This chapter is intended for DoubleSpace users who are interested in the technical aspects of the program.

We'll discuss the command line interface to DoubleSpace. You'll also learn how to use or manipulate DoubleSpace drives from within your own programs via system calls to the DoubleSpace API (Application Program Interface).

Command Lines

You can access DoubleSpace directly from the DOS level, without going through the program's menus and dialog boxes. This means that you can use DoubleSpace calls within batch files, or even build them into your own programs using the Shell command of a programming language.

The following is a list of the available command sequences:

```
DBLSPACE /COMPRESS
```

Compresses the files on a hard drive or diskette or other removable storage media. DoubleSpace cannot compress a drive that's completely full. Your boot drive must have at least 1.7 Meg of free space. Other hard drives require a minimum of 1 Meg of free space. A diskette must have at least 200K free. DoubleSpace cannot compress a 360K diskette.

Syntax

DBLSPACE /COMPRESS Drive1: [/NEWDRIVE=Drive2:] [/RESERVE=Size]

Parameters

Drive1: Specifies drive to be compressed.

Switches

/COMPRESS: Compresses the specified drive. This switch can be shortened to /COM.

Chapter Six

/NEWDRIVE=Drive2: Specifies drive letter of new, uncompressed drive. The /NEWDRIVE parameter is optional. If it is omitted, DoubleSpace assigns the next available drive letter. This switch can be shortened to /NEW.

/RESERVE=Size: Indicates how much space (in megabytes) should remain uncompressed. The uncompressed space resides on the new, uncompressed drive. This switch can be shortened to /RES.

Examples

```
DBLSPACE /COMPRESS D:
```

Compresses drive D:. Since the amount of space that is to remain uncompressed isn't indicated, DoubleSpace leaves a 2 Meg-area uncompressed. Since no drive letter is specified for the new, uncompressed drive, DoubleSpace assigns it the next available letter.

```
DBLSPACE /COMPRESS /NEWDRIVE=F: /RESERVE=4
```

Compresses the current drive. Assigns the new uncompressed drive the letter F: and leaves 4 Meg uncompressed space there.

DBLSPACE /CREATE

Creates a new compressed drive by using the free space on an uncompressed drive.

Syntax

```
DBLSPACE /CREATE Drive1: [/NEWDRIVE=Drive2:] [/SIZE=Size |
/RESERVE=Size]
```

Parameters

Drive1: Provides the uncompressed drive that contains the storage space for creating the new drive.

Inside DoubleSpace

Chapter Six

Switches

/CREATE: Creates a new compressed drive by using the free space on the uncompressed Drive1. This switch can be shortened to /CR.

/NEWDRIVE=Drive2: Specifies the letter of the new compressed drive. If it is omitted, DoubleSpace assigns the new drive the next available letter. This switch can be shortened to /NEW.

/RESERVE=Size: Specifies how many megabytes of free space DoubleSpace should reserve on the uncompressed drive. To make the compressed drive as large as possible, specify a size of 0 here.

/SIZE=Size: Specifies the total size of a compressed drive in megabytes. This is the amount of space on the uncompressed drive that will be assigned to the compressed drive. The /SIZE switch can be shortened to /SI.

Examples

```
DBLSPACE /CREATE E: /RESERVE=0
```

Creates, on drive E:, a new compressed drive that uses the entire space available.

```
DBLSPACE /CREATE E: /SIZE=10
```

Creates, on drive E:, a new compressed drive that uses 10 Meg of the space available.

```
DBLSPACE /CREATE D: /RESERVE=2.75
```

Creates, on drive D:, a new compressed drive and leaves 2.75 Meg uncompressed.

> **Note**
> Only one of the two switches /RESERVE and /SIZE can be specified. If both are omitted, DoubleSpace reserves 2 Meg of the available space. The /RESERVE switch can be shortened to /RE.

Inside DoubleSpace

Chapter Six

DBLSPACE /DEFRAGMENT

Defragments the specified compressed drive.

Syntax

```
DBLSPACE /DEFRAGMENT [Drive:]
```

Parameters

Drive: Specifies the drive to be defragmented. This parameter is optional. If no drive is specified, DoubleSpace defragments the current drive.

Switches

/DEFRAGMENT: Tells DoubleSpace to defragment the specified drive. This switch can be shortened to /DEF.

DBLSPACE /DELETE

Deletes the specified compressed drive and its compressed volume file.

Syntax

```
DBLSPACE /DELETE Drive:
```

Parameters

Drive: Specifies the drive to be deleted.

Switches

/DELETE: Deletes the specified drive. This switch can be shortened to /DEL.

> **Warning**
> Deleting a compressed drive deletes all the files contained on the drive.

> **Note**
> DoubleSpace won't let you delete drive C:

Inside DoubleSpace

Chapter Six

DBLSPACE /FORMAT

Formats the specified compressed drive.

Syntax

```
DBLSPACE /FORMAT Drive:
```

Parameters

Drive: Specifies the drive to be formatted.

> **Warning**
> Formatting a compressed drive deletes all the files contained on the drive. You cannot unformat a drive that has been formatted with DBLSPACE /FORMAT.

Switches

/FORMAT: Instructs DoubleSpace to format the specified compressed drive. This switch can be shortened to /F.

> **Note**
> DoubleSpace won't let you format drive C:

DBLSPACE /INFO

Displays information about a compressed drive:

- Amount of free memory
- Amount of used memory
- Name of compressed volume file
- Actual and estimated compression ratio

Syntax

```
DBLSPACE [/INFO] Drive:
```

Inside DoubleSpace

Chapter Six

Parameters

   Drive: Specifies the compressed drive for which information is needed.

Switches

   /INFO: Tells DoubleSpace to display information on the specified drive. You can omit this switch if you specify a drive letter.

DBLSPACE /LIST

Lists all drives present on your computer and provides a brief description. Network drives aren't displayed.

Syntax

```
DBLSPACE /LIST
```

Switches

   /LIST: Tells DoubleSpace to display a list of your computer's local drives. This switch can be shortened to /L.

DBLSPACE /MOUNT

Establishes a link between the compressed volume file and a drive letter, so you can work with the files contained in the volume file.

Syntax

```
DBLSPACE /MOUNT[=nnn] Drive1: [/NEWDRIVE=Drive2:]
```

Parameters

   Drive1:   Specifies the drive containing the compressed volume file to be mounted.

Inside DoubleSpace

Chapter Six

Switches

/MOUNT=nnn: Tells DoubleSpace to mount the compressed volume file named with the parameter "nnn." For example, to mount the file DBLSPACE.001, specify "/MOUNT=001." If the parameter nnn is omitted, DoubleSpace attempts to mount the compressed volume file DBLSPACE.000. The /MOUNT switch can be shortened to /MO.

/NEWDRIVE=Drive2: Specifies letter to be assigned to a new compressed drive. If no letter is specified, DoubleSpace assigns the next available letter to the new drive. This switch can be shortened to /NEW.

DBLSPACE /RATIO

Changes the estimated compression ratio of the specified drive.

Syntax

```
DBLSPACE /RATIO[=r.r] [Drive: | /ALL]
```

Parameters

Drive: Specifies the drive whose estimated compression ratio you want to change. You can specify a letter or the /ALL switch, but not both. If neither is specified, DoubleSpace applies the change to the current drive.

Switches

/RATIO=r.r: Changes the estimated compression ratio of the specified drive. If the ratio must be changed to a particular number, enter the desired number. Permissible values are from 1.0 to 16.0.

If a value isn't specified, DoubleSpace changes the estimated compression ratio to the actual compression ratio. This switch can be shortened to /RA.

Chapter Six

/ALL: Applies the change in compression ratio to all currently mounted compressed drives.

DBLSPACE /SIZE

Shrinks or expands a compressed drive.

Syntax

```
DBLSPACE /SIZE[=Size1 | /RESERVE=Size2] Drive:
```

Parameters

Drive: Specifies the drive whose size must be changed.

Switches

/SIZE=Size1: Changes the size of the specified drive to Size1. The /SIZE switch can be shortened to /SI.

/RESERVE=Size2: Specifies how many megabytes of free space the uncompressed (host) drive should have after DoubleSpace has changed the size of the compressed drive. The /RESERVE switch can be shortened to /RES.

Examples

```
DBLSPACE /SIZE=60 C:
```

The compressed volume file on drive C: is adjusted so 60 Meg of the host drive is used.

```
DBLSPACE /SIZE /RESERVE=20 E:
```

The compressed volume file on drive E: is adjusted so 20 Meg remain free on the host drive.

```
DBLSPACE /SIZE /RESERVE=0 C:
```

Adjusts the compressed volume file on drive C: to the maximum possible size.

> **Note**
> You can use either the /SIZE parameter or the /RESERVE option to indicate the new drive size, but not both. If you omit both, DoubleSpace makes the drive as small as possible.

Inside DoubleSpace

Chapter Six

DBLSPACE /UNMOUNT

Unmounts a compressed drive, so it can no longer be referenced through its drive letter. You cannot unmount drive C:.

Syntax

```
DBLSPACE /UNMOUNT [Drive:]
```

Parameters

Drive: Specifies the drive to be unmounted. This parameter is optional. If it is omitted, DoubleSpace unmounts the current drive.

Switches

/UNMOUNT: Unmounts the given compressed drive. This switch can be shortened to /U.

DBLSPACE /?

Displays help information for using DoubleSpace at the DOS level.

DoubleSpace help screen

Inside DoubleSpace

Chapter Six

Extensions in DOS 6.2

DOS 6.2 has several extensions at the command line level that allow you to change the contents of DBLSPACE.INI:

> DBLSPACE /AUTOMOUNT=0|1|A...Z

Enables or disables automatic mounting and unmounting of DoubleSpace 6.2 compressed diskettes.

Parameters

0	Disables the Automount function and saves main memory.
1	Activates Automount (the default setting).
A..Z	Specifies the drive to be automounted.

> DBLSPACE /DOUBLEGUARD=0|1

Enables or disables the DoubleGuard function.

Parameters

0	Disables DoubleGuard.
1	Enables DoubleGuard (default).

> DLBSPACE /LASTDRIVE=x

Provides the last drive letter available to DoubleSpace as "x."

> DBLSPACE /MAXFILEFRAGMENTS=n

Provides the maximum allowable number of file fragments as "n."

Inside DoubleSpace

Chapter Six

```
DBLSPACE /MAXREMOVABLEDRIVES=n
```

Provides the maximum number of compressed drives as "n."

```
DBLSPACE /ROMSERVER=0|1
```

Enables or disables the ROM BIOS MRCI (Microsoft Real-time Compression Interface).

Parameters

0   Disables the function.

1   Enables the function.

You can only use the ROM server if your hardware supports the MRCI.

```
DBLSPACE /SWITCHES=F|N|FN
```

DoubleSpace 6.2 can be deactivated during system startup by pressing F5 or F8 when the "Starting MS-DOS..." prompt appears. This lets you operate without DoubleSpace, which can be useful for performing system checks or when running memory-intensive applications.

Parameters

N   Speeds up the boot process by shortening the time, during which you can interrupt, with the control switches.

F   Prevents you from disabling DoubleSpace. You can still use F8 to step through the CONFIG.SYS and AUTOEXEC.BAT commands one at a time, or F5 to bypass both start files. DoubleSpace will still be activated.

FN   Combines the effects of the first two parameters.

Inside DoubleSpace

Chapter Six

DBLSPACE drive1:/HOST=drive2

Changes the host drive designator.

Parameters

    drive1   The current value.

    drive2   The new value.

DBLSPACE.SYS

Determines the position of DBLSPACE.BIN in working memory. DBLSPACE.BIN is the part of MS-DOS that lets you access your compressed drive. When you switch on your computer, MS-DOS loads DBLSPACE.BIN and other operating system functions before executing the commands in CONFIG.SYS and AUTOEXEC.BAT. DBLSPACE.BIN is first loaded to Conventional memory, since it's loaded before the device driver that permits access to upper memory.

When you install DoubleSpace, the program adds a DEVICE command to your CONFIG.SYS file for the device driver DBLSPACE.SYS. To move DBLSPACE.BIN to Upper memory, you must change the DEVICE command for DBLSPACE.SYS to a DEVICEHIGH command.

Syntax

```
DEVICE = [Drive:][Path]DBLSPACE.SYS /MOVE
DEVICEHIGH = [Drive:][Path]DBLSPACE.SYS /MOVE
```

Switches

    /MOVE: Moves DBLSPACE.BIN from Conventional to Upper memory.

Parameters

    [Drive:][Path]:   Indicates where the DBLSPACE.SYS file resides.

Inside DoubleSpace

Chapter Six

The DoubleSpace API

DoubleSpace also includes a documented API (Application Programming Interface), which is in the DBLSPACE.BIN file. The API is an interface to programming languages. Programmers can use the API for designing an alternative DoubleSpace interface or for file management programs and shells. In this chapter, we'll explain how an API call is made and which system calls are involved.

Calling methods

The DoubleSpace API has two calling methods. The first runs via the INT 2Fh Multiplex Service, an interrupt that permits a simple call without a specific drive designator. The second runs via an Input/Output Control Interface (IOCtl), and uses the DOS kernel. This sets certain system flags that prevent a duplicate call of DBLSPACE.BIN and a subsequent system abort. The second, more complex method can be used only for certain calls.

INT 2Fh calls

The following are the assembler instructions for an INT 2Fh call:

```
MOV AX,4a11h      AX=DoubleSpace INT 2Fh multiplex-
number
MOV BX,function   BX=API function number
... set other registers
INT 2Fh    Interrupt call. Result in AX
OR AX,AX   Check if successful
JNZ error  Error
;;Successful
```

IOCtl calls

IOCtl functions are activated via the call IOCtl Read Control Data from Block Device Driver (INT 21h, Function 44h, Subfunction 04h) with a DS:DX-pointer to a function buffer.

It looks like this:

Inside DoubleSpace

Chapter Six

```
MD_STAMP EQU 'DM'
dspacket STRUC
dspStamp DW ?      Identification
dspCommand DB ?    Command 'F' or 'I'
dspResult DW ?     Result 'OK'
dspPadding DB 5 DUP (?)
dspacket ENDS
dsp struc <MD_STAMP,'F','??',>
...
MOV AX,4404h       IOCtl Read command
MOV BL,drive       Drive letter
MOV CX,SIZE dsp    Packet length
MOV dsp.dspResult,'??'  Reset result
INT 21h            Interrupt call
CMP dsp.dspREsult,'OK'  Check if successful
JNE error   Unsuccessful
;;Successful
```

API functions

Now we'll describe the individual functions. At the start of every API call sequence, the call DSGetVersion must be executed to determine whether DBLSPACE.BIN is resident in memory. If it isn't, any other calls will lead to system aborts.

DSGetVersion

This function provides the DoubleSpace version number and also indicates whether DBLSPACE.BIN is resident in memory. This function also checks for the letter of the first DoubleSpace drive and the total number of compressed drives in the system.

Call

```
MOV AX,4A11h
MOV BX,0
INT 2Fh
```

Results:

AX=0   Successful

BX=0x444D ('M','D')

Inside DoubleSpace

Chapter Six

CL=First drive letter (based on A:=0)

CH=Number of compressed drives

DX=Internal version number, to distinguish between DBLSPACE.BIN, IO.SYS and DBLSPACE.EXE.

DSFlushCache (IOCtl='F')

DBLSPACE.BIN works with internal cache memory areas for data and FAT (File Allocation Table). This function forces DoubleSpace to save the cache contents to the compressed volume file.

The dspCommand field must be set to 046h.

DSFlushAndInvalidateCache (IOCtl='I')

This function not only saves the cache contents to the volume file, but empties out the cache itself. It should be called before optimizing, defragmenting, or similar operations are performed directly on the volume file.

The dspCommand field must be set to 049h.

DSGetDriveMapping

Provides information about a particular compressed drive, for example, its host drive and number.

Call

```
MOV AX,4A11h
MOV BX,1
MOV DL,drive number (based on 0)
INT 2Fh
```

Results

AX=0 if successful

BL AND 7Fh=Host drive

BL AND 80h=1 if compressed, 0 if not

BH=Number of the compressed drive (0...254)

DSSwapDrive

Swaps drive designators between the host drive and compressed volume file. This call should only occur through DBLSPACE.EXE if the entire drive is compressed.

Call

```
MOV AX,4A11h
MOV BX,2
MOV DL,drive number (based on 0)
INT 2Fh
```

Results

AX=0 if successful

AX=error number (see explanation on page 223)

DSGetEntryPoints

Provides entry point addresses of the DBLSPACE.BIN driver, so a cache program, for example, can reroute DBLSPACE calls.

Call

```
MOV AX,4A11h
MOV BX,3
MOV DL,drive number (based on 0)
INT 2Fh
```

Results

CL=driver or error number

ES:DI=device driver interrupt

ES:SI=strategy routine

DSSetEntryPoints

Reroutes DBLSPACE calls (e.g., to a cache program).

Inside DoubleSpace

Chapter Six

Call

```
MOV AX,4A11h
MOV BX,4
MOV CL,drive number (based on 0)
MOV DL,driver number for rerouted driver
MOV DH,0
MOV ES,segment for new driver
MOV DI,offset for interrupt
MOV SI,offset for strategy routine
INT 2Fh
```

Results

CL=driver number or error

DSActivateDrive

Opens a compressed volume file as a drive. The call for this function is very complex. Instead, use the following program call line:

`dblspace.exe /mount[=seq]Hostdrive [/NEWDRIVE=Driveletter]`

DSDeactivateDrive

Closes a compressed drive.

Call

```
MOV AX,4A11h
MOV BX,6
MOV DL,drive number (based on 0)
INT 2Fh
```

Results

AX=0 or error

Drive is closed.

Chapter Six

DSGetDriveSpace

Indicates the number of sectors and free sectors on a compressed drive.

Call

```
MOV AX,4A11h
MOV BX,7
MOV DL,drive number (based on 0)
INT 2Fh
```

Results

AX=0 or error

DWORD PTR DS:SI[0]=total number of sectors

DWORD PTR DS:SI[4]=number of free sectors

DSGetFileFragmentSpace

Provides the number of fragmentations on the compressed volume file and the permissible number remaining.

Call

```
MOV AX,4A11h
MOV BX,8
INT 2Fh
```

Results

AX=0 or error

BX=maximum number of fragmentations

CX=permissible number of fragmentations remaining

DSGetExtraInfo

Number of compressed drives.

Inside DoubleSpace

Chapter Six

Call

```
MOV AX,4A11h
MOV BX,9
INT 2Fh
```

Results

AX=0 or error

CL=number of compressed drives or, more precisely, the number of disk units allocated by DBLSPACE.BIN.

Errors

Most functions return an error code in Register AX if the action was not successful. For INT 2Fh calls, the following errors are possible:

100h	Unknown function
101h	Invalid drive number
102h	Not a compressed drive
103h	Host drive letter already swapped
104h	Host drive letter not swapped

The two IOCtl calls recognize the following additional errors:

1	Drive letter not available for DoubleSpace
2	Drive letter already in use
3	No more compressed drives allowed
4	Compressed volume file is too fragmented

Compressed volume file structure

The following table shows the structure of a compressed volume file:

Chapter Six

Name	Offset	Size	Description
MDBPB	0	1	Maximum storage capacity
BitFAT	1	~	Indicates sector in use or free
Reserved1	1	1	Reserved
MDFAT	...	~	Position of sectors for a cluster
Reserved2	...	1	Reserved
Boot Sector	...	1	Boot sector (For compatibility only, not functional for starting)
Reserved3	...	~	Reserved
FAT	...	~	File Allocation Table
Root Directory	...	32	Root directory
Reserved4	...	2	Reserved
Sector Heap	...	60	Overview of occupied sectors
2nd Stamp	...	1+	Internal stamp

~ represents variable size

Chapter 7

Glossary

Contents

Archive 227
Access rights 227
AUTOEXEC.BAT 227
Backup 227
Batch file 228
Boot sector 228
CHKDSK 228
CVF 228
Conventional memory 228
Current directory 229
Current drive 229
DEFRAG 229
Defragmenting 229
DBLSPACE 230
Expanded memory 230
Extended memory 230
FDISK 231
High memory 231
Logical drives 231
MEM 231
MEMMAKER 231
MSBACKUP 232
Partition 232
RAM disk 232
Upper memory 232
Virtual drive 233

Glossary

Chapter Seven

This chapter covers important terms used in working with MS-DOS and data compression.

Archive

A compressed file which is designed to save space on your hard drive. An archive always contains at least one file.

Access rights

Rights of a user to use programs or data. Access rights can be set up and changed by the supervisor with the SYSCON utility program. In Novell, you can specify access rights individually for each user and each directory. Along with DOS attributes such as "Read-Only" or "Hidden", there are also special rights for opening or closing files and creating subdirectories.

AUTOEXEC.BAT

Abbreviation for AUTOEXECute BATch file. This text file contains a series of commands stored in a group. Immediately after you switch on the PC, the computer searches for an AUTOEXEC.BAT file. If one exists, the commands in this file execute automatically.

AUTOEXEC.BAT commands often include the display of the version of DOS in use (VER), the DATE and TIME commands.

The AUTOEXEC.BAT file is a special form of batch file. Like all other batch files, AUTOEXEC.BAT can also be called and executed directly from the system prompt.

Backup

To copy important data and program files to a removable storage device (such as a floppy diskette) so it can be kept in a safe off-site location.

A backup is the copy of a program or document file made for archival purposes.

Glossary

Chapter Seven

Batch file

A file containing a collection of commands (see *AUTOEXEC.BAT*). MS-DOS executes these commands in sequence when you type the name of the file.

Batch files are created using the COPY CON command (e.g., COPY CON FILE.BAT), the MS-DOS Editor, a word processing program, or the EDLIN (can be found on the Supplemental Disk from Microsoft) line editor. The .BAT extension must be included with any batch filename.

Boot sector

The sector on which MS-DOS is located on your hard drive.

CHKDSK

Pronounced "check-disk", use this DOS command to check the status of your hard drive or disk drive. It then displays a status report showing any errors found in the MS-DOS filing system, which consists of the file allocation table (FAT) and directories.

Although you can also use CHKDSK to fix disk errors, the ScanDisk program is the recommended method of fixing drive problems.

CVF

An acronym for Compressed Volume File.

Conventional memory

Conventional memory is memory below the 640K limit. Because this memory area has been reserved for DOS programs and data since the development of the first PCs, it can be used by programs without restrictions or compatibility problems. All other forms of memory have special requirements for programs that use these memory types or else result in incompatibilities.

Glossary

Chapter Seven

Due to internal management and procedures, it's not the entire amount of conventional memory, but the largest available memory block that provides the most important limitation for programs. Most programs use only the largest available block; other memory blocks are ignored.

Current directory

To access a file or a directory, DOS uses the current directory. You make a directory current by showing the position relative to the current directory using the CD.. command.

A second method is to use the CD NAME command. You must indicate the drive (letter and colon) and then the path through the subdirectories separated by the backslash.

Current drive

The standard drive or current drive is the drive to which all disk commands of the computer apply. Usually, and especially for systems with only one drive, this is drive A:. If two drives are available, the second drive can be selected with B:. This command can be reversed with A:. The hard drive can be selected with C:. The standard drive is displayed in the system prompt.

DEFRAG

Reorganizes the files on a disk to optimize disk performance. Do not use DEFRAG when Windows is running.

Defragmenting

Since data are constantly being deleted and resaved on computers, the space on the hard drive is not filled up in sequence with files. As a result, areas with and without data of varying size break up or "fragment" the contiguous free space on the hard drive.

To create an optimum area of contiguous free memory on the hard drive, you can use special defragmentation programs like DEFRAG, which comes supplied with MS-DOS 6. Defragmentation programs reorganize the allocated memory areas to create a contiguous area of allocated and free memory on the hard drive.

Glossary

Chapter Seven

DBLSPACE

Compresses hard disk drives or floppy disks, and configures drives that were compressed by using DoubleSpace.

Expanded memory

Expanded memory is a method of breaking through the basic 640K limit of conventional memory. This limit results from the fact that a PC/XT can only process addresses of up to 1 Meg. The area up to 640K is reserved for conventional memory; the rest contains special expansions (e.g., memory for a special graphics expansion, EGA or VGA card) or is free.

Expanded memory is additional available memory that is below the 1 Meg memory address limit. Such memory could be present on special memory expansion cards, for example. Special electronic circuitry makes this kind of memory available to the computer in "small amounts". MS-DOS or application programs are then able to use this memory. Such programs must support working with expanded memory.

MS-DOS is not able to use expanded memory directly, but some auxiliary programs can store data in this kind of memory. For example, SMARTDRV, the program for speeding up hard drives and RAMDRIVE are able to use expanded memory. The BUFFERS and FASTOPEN commands also use expanded memory. Many application programs can also work with expanded memory.

Extended memory

Extended memory is memory present beyond the 1 Meg limit of memory that can be used by MS-DOS. Only ATs (286, 386 etc.) are able to use this type of memory. Expanded memory is not "inserted in a window" via special hardware and software the way expanded memory is, but can be used by different programs without additional hardware or software.

Extended memory can by used by MS-DOS for the RAMDRIVE RAM disk and SMARTDRV.

Glossary

Chapter Seven

FDISK

Use this command to start the FDISK program. It configures a hard disk for use with MS-DOS. FDISK displays several menus to help you partition your hard disk(s) for MS-DOS.

High memory

High Memory is the first 64K of extended memory. Unlike the rest of extended memory, high memory can also be used in real mode on an AT without difficulty. High memory is part of XMS memory and is managed by HIMEM.SYS. MS-DOS can relocate a large portion of the DOS kernel to high memory, freeing up more conventional memory.

Logical drives

Logical drives are parts of the hard drive that can be addressed by a separate drive letter. They are defined in an extended DOS partition. In this way, it is possible to divide a hard drive into several drives when formatting with FDISK.

The need for these "logical drives" comes from a time prior to MS-DOS 4.0, when MS-DOS was only able to process hard drives with up to 32 Meg capacity. The solution was to divide larger hard drives into several logical drives.

For compatibility reasons, there are also logical drives in newer versions of MS-DOS, although hard drives of up to 2,048 Meg can easily be managed as a single drive.

MEM

Use this DOS command to display the amount of used and free memory on your computer. The MEM command can also be used to display information about allocated memory areas, free memory areas, and programs that are loaded into memory.

MEMMAKER

Use this DOS command to start the MEMMAKER program. This program optimizes the memory of your computer by moving device drivers and memory-resident programs to upper memory.

Glossary

Chapter Seven

To use MEMMAKER, your computer must have an 80386 or 80486 processor and extended memory.

> **Warning**
> Do not use MEMMAKER when you're in Windows.

MSBACKUP

Use this command to run Microsoft Backup for MS-DOS. It backs up or restores one or more files from one disk onto another.

Partition

DOS can work with a hard drive only if it has a DOS partition (a DOS area). By dividing the hard drive into several partitions (areas) with FDISK, you can use another operating system on the hard drive as well as DOS (e.g., OS/2 with the HPS = High Performance System or Unix).

MS-DOS can boot from the hard drive only if the DOS area is startable (primary partition). A second area can be set up as an extended partition with one or more logical drives.

RAM disk

An area created in RAM by a program to act as a disk drive temporarily on the DOS disk.

Since it is not a mechanical device, the RAM disk allows very fast file access, but loses all data when you switch off your PC.

PC users with only one disk drive will find the RAM disk extremely helpful. Anything can be kept in a RAM disk, provided the files do not exceed the memory limits.

Upper memory

Upper memory is the memory between 640K and 1 Meg; this is also called "reserved memory" in other operating systems. Both names describe aspects of this memory type. Upper memory is above 640K, or conventional memory. Upper memory is also "reserved" for video display, the BIOS and expansions.

Glossary

Chapter Seven

However, usually this memory area is not allocated by expansion cards, so that you can install an EMS window (page frame) for expanded memory there. MS-DOS attempts to fill free areas on computers with 386 processors with extended memory and then use it as upper memory for swapping TSR programs and device drivers. To do this, you need a 386 or above and a special device driver (EMM386.EXE).

Virtual drive

An installed RAM disk.

DoubleSpace Without the DoubleTalk

Index

A

Access rights 227
Application Programming Interface . 217–224
    See also DoubleSpace API
Archive 227
AUTOEXEC.BAT 227

B

BACKUP 39–70
    Restoring data after BACKUP ....
    .... 50-54, 63-65
Backup 227
Batch file 228
Boot sector 228

C

Cache programs
    Using with DoubleSpace 124
    Using with Stacker 179
CHK files
    Removing 87
CHKDSK 36–37, 228
Compressed drives
    Defragmenting in DoubleSpace 111
    Deleting in DoubleSpace 110–111
    DoubleSpace 97–101
    Formatting in DoubleSpace 109–110
    Managing in DoubleSpace 101–115
    Managing in Stacker 157–175
    Managing in Stacker (DOS version) ....
    157–169
    Using in Stacker 152–156
    Using in Stacker (DOS version) 153–155
    Using in Stacker (Windows version) ....
    155–156
Compressed files
    Using with DoubleSpace 126
    Using with Stacker 181
Compressed Volume Files 17–18
Compressing a hard drive 29–79
Compression factor 18–20
Compression ratios 20–21
    Changing in DoubleSpace 108–109
    Changing in Stacker (DOS version) ....
    164–165
    Changing in Stacker (Windows version) ...
    171–186
Compression speed 21–22
Conventional memory 228
Current directory 229
Current drive 229
CVF 228
    See also Compressed Volume Files

D

Data compression 15–26
    Advantages 6–8
    Before compressing your hard drive . 29–79
    Compressed Volume Files 17–18
    Compression factor 18–20
    Compression ratios 20–21
    Compression speed 21–22
    Cross-linked file clusters 23
    Data security 25–26
    Defined 3–5
    Disadvantages 6–8
    Fragmentation 22–23
    Host drives 18

DoubleSpace Without the DoubleTalk

Index

Introduction 3–12
Logical drives 15–16
Memory management 25
Memory types 23–25
Methods 5–6
Online compression 15–26
Partitions 16
Physical drives 15–16
Programs 8–9
RAM drives 17
Selecting a compression program 9–10
System requirements 10–12
Uses for data compression 4–5
Data compression methods 5–6
   Offline compression 5–6
   Online compression 6
Data compression programs 8–9
   Selecting a program 9–10
Data security 25–26
DBLSPACE 230
DBLSPACE.INF 118–122
   See also DoubleSpace
DBLSPACE.INI 121–122
   See also DoubleSpace
DEFRAG 37–39, 229
Defragmenting 229
   DoubleSpace 87–88, 111
   Stacker (DOS version) 166–168
   Stacker (Windows version) 173–175
Diskettes
   Compressing in DoubleSpace 112–116
DOS DEFRAG
   Using with DoubleSpace 128
   Using with Stacker 181–201
DoubleSpace 83–132
   API 217–224
   Changing compression ratio 108–109
   Changing drive size 105–108
   Commands 205–214
   Compressing diskettes 112–116
   DBLSPACE.INF 118–121
   DBLSPACE.INI 121–122
   Defragmenting compressed drives 111
   Deleting compressed drives 110–111
   DOS 6.2 additions 122–123
   Error messages 128–131
   Formatting compressed drives 109–110
   Installation 83–96
   Managing compressed drives 101–115
   Menu bar 102–105
   Optimizing hard drives 116–122
   Removing 131–132
   Uncompressing drives (DOS 6.2) 132
   Using compressed drives 97–101
   Using with cache programs 124
   Using with compressed files 126
   Using with DOS DEFRAG 128
   Using with drive device drivers 126
   Using with EXTDISK.SYS 125–126
   Using with Novel networks 127–128
   Using with other applications 123–128
   Using with Windows Flexboot System ......
       126
   Using with Windows swap files 124–125
DoubleSpace API 217–224
   Calling methods 217
DoubleSpace commands 205–214
   DBLSPACE/COMPRESS 205–206
   DBLSPACE/CREATE 206–208
   DBLSPACE/DEFRAGMENT 208
   DBLSPACE/DELETE 208–209
   DBLSPACE/FORMAT 209
   DBLSPACE/INFO 209–210
   DBLSPACE/LIST 210
   DBLSPACE/MOUNT 210–211
   DBLSPACE/RATIO 211–212
   DBLSPACE/SIZE 212–213
   DBLSPACE/UNMOUNT 213–214
   DOS 6.2 extensions 214–216
DoubleSpace commands (DOS 6.2) ... 214–216
   DBLSPACE/AUTOMOUNT 214
   DBLSPACE/DBLSPACE.SYS 216
   DBLSPACE/DOUBLEGUARD 214
   DBLSPACE/drive1:/HOST=drive2 216
   DBLSPACE/LASTDRIVE 214
   DBLSPACE/MAXFILEFRAGMENTS ....
       214–215

DoubleSpace Without the DoubleTalk

Index

DBLSPACE/MAXREMOVABLEDRIVES 215
DBLSPACE/ROMSERVER 215
DBLSPACE/SWITCHES 215–216
DoubleSpace installation 83–96
    Checking partitions 83–84
    Converting compressed drives 95–96
    Defragmenting 87–88
    Deleting unnecessary files 85–87
    Optimizing memory 95
    Removing CHK files 87
    Starting the installation 88–95
Drive device driver
    Using with DoubleSpace 126
Drive size
    Changing in DoubleSpace 105–108
    Changing in Stacker (DOS version) 160–164

E

Error messages
    DoubleSpace 128–131
    Stacker 181–182
Expanded memory 230
EXTDISK.SYS device driver
    Using with DoubleSpace 125–126
Extended memory 230

F

FDISK 29–34, 231
FORMAT 34–36
Fragmentation 22–23

G

Glossary 227–233

H

Hard drives
    Compressing 29–79
    Optimizing in DoubleSpace 116–122
    Optimizing in Stacker 175–179
High memory 231
Host drives 18

L

Logical drives 15–16, 231

M

Managing compressed drives
    Stacker (DoubleSpace) 101-115
    Stacker (Windows version) 169–175
MEM 70–71, 231
MEMMAKER 72–78, 231
Memory management 25
Memory types 23–25
MSBACKUP 232
MSBACKUP for DOS 39–50
MSBACKUP for Windows 54–62

N

Novell networks
    Using with DoubleSpace 127–128

238 DoubleSpace Without the DoubleTalk

Index

O

Offline compression 5–6
Online compression 6, 15–26

P

Partition 16, 232
    Cross-linked file clusters 23
Physical drives 15–16

R

RAM disk 232
RAM drives 17
Removing DoubleSpace 131–132
Removing Stacker 183–184
RESTORE
    Used with BACKUP 65–70
Restoring data after BACKUP ... 50–54, 63–65

S

ScanDisk 78–79
Stacker 135–201
    Command lines 185–201
    Converting a DoubleSpace drive .. 150–152
    Error messages 181–182
    Installation 135–152
    Managing compressed drives 157–175
    Optimizing hard drives 175–179
    Removing 183–184
    Stacker Tuner 177–179
    Uncompressing drives 184–185
    Using compressed drives 152–156
    Using with cache programs 179
    Using with compressed files 181
    Using with DOS DEFRAG 181–201
    Using with other applications 179–181
    Using with Windows swap files 180
Stacker (DOS version)
    Changing compression ratio 164–165
    Changing drive size 160–164
    Checking the drive 168–169
    Defragmenting drives 166–168
    Interface 158–160
    Managing compressed drives 157–169
    Using compressed drives 153–155
Stacker (Windows version) 169–175
    Changing compression ratio 171–186
    Defragmenting files 173–175
    Managing compressed drives 169–175
    Stackometer 170–171
    Starting 170–171
    Using compressed drives 155–156
Stacker commands 185–201
    Check 186–187
    Create 187–188
    DCONVERT 188–189
    Ed 189–190
    Passwd 190–191
    Preview 191–192
    Removdrv 192
    Report 192–193
    SAttrib 193–194
    SDefrag 194–196
    SDir 196–197
    Setup 197–198
    Stacker 198
    Tuner 198–199
    Unstack 199–201
Stacker Tuner 177–179
    See also Stacker
Stackometer
    See Stacker (Windows version)
System requirements for data compression ...
    10–12

Index

U

Uncompressing drives
    Stacker 184–185
Upper memory 232

V

Virtual drive 233

W

Windows NT Flexboot System
    Using with DoubleSpace 126
Windows swap file
    Using with DoubleSpace 124–125
    Using with Stacker 180

PC catalog

Order Toll Free 1-800-451-4319
Books and Software

Abacus

To order direct call Toll Free 1-800-451-4319

In US and Canada add $5.00 shipping and handling. Foreign orders add $13.00 per item.
Michigan residents add 4% sales tax.

Developers Series books are for professional software developers who require in-depth technical information and programming techniques.

AutoCAD 12 Programming

AutoCAD 12 Programming will teach you how to integrate special custom functions and commands into your AutoCAD system. **AutoCAD 12 Programming** presents the many options of AutoCAD programming in a well-founded, yet easy to understand format. This guide includes thorough descriptions of how to create custom work environments and custom menus. **AutoCAD 12 Programming** explains BATCH programming (for user defined startup of Auto CAD 12), creating Script files (for specific drawing sequences) and programming custom commands with AutoLISP or ADS.

Also includes:
- Overview of AutoCAD 12
- Installation tips
- Prototype drawing and output functions
- Script programming
- AutoLISP, menus and commands
- AutoCAD Development System
- Practical information to adapt AutoCAD to your requirements.

AutoCAD 12 Programming includes a companion disk that contains programming examples and ready to use menus.

Author: Christian Immler
ISBN: 1-55755-173-1
Order Item: #B173
Suggested retail price: $44.95 US/ $54.95 CAN with companion diskette

To order direct call Toll Free 1-800-451-4319

In US and Canada add $5.00 shipping and handling. Foreign orders add $13.00 per item. Michigan residents add 4% sales tax.

Entertainment for All Ages

Links™ is the most popular golf simulation on the market today.
Links - The Pro's Tour Guide
teaches you how to take advantage of all the unique and powerful features of the Links golf simulation. This guide teaches you about the different types of golf clubs and how to select the correct club. You'll learn how to deal with outside variables such as wind and green conditions, and how to improve your short and long game and much more.

Includes information on:
- Using special features of Links, The Challenge of Golf, Links 386 Pro and Microsoft Golf simulations and getting the most from Links
- Beginner's basic training for playing golf
- Course guides with diagrams and distances
- Helpful hints and tips for running Links on your PC
- Chapter of golf terms
- Distance and condition tables

You'll learn how to improve your scores step by step. This book dedicates a whole chapter to thorough explanations of golf terms, including handicap, birdie, bogey, etc. Also includes an explanation of the Control Panel functions of Links.

Authors: Rolf Meusel, Robert Kniest
ISBN: 1-55755-180-4
Order Item: B180
Price: $16.95 U.S./ CDN: $21.95

To order direct call Toll Free 1-800-451-4319

In US and Canada add $5.00 shipping and handling. Foreign orders add $13.00 per item. Michigan residents add 4% sales tax.

Multimedia Presentation

Multimedia Mania

explores the evolving multimedia explosion. This book begins by explaining what the term multimedia means, continues with valuable information necessary for setting up a complete multimedia system, then provides instructions on creating multimedia presentations. **Multimedia Mania** also includes information about popular multimedia programs.

Multimedia Mania will guide you through workshops helping you develop professional presentations. The companion CD-ROM contains example programs and samples of techniques discussed in the book allowing you to gain practical experience working with multimedia.

Multimedia Mania also covers:

- ◆ Audio Technology: sound boards and sound recording
- ◆ CD and CD-ROM technology
- ◆ Windows 3.1 and its impact on multimedia
- ◆ Capturing and editing pictures
- ◆ Animation techniques
- ◆ Electronic Composition - the world of MIDI

Order Item # B166. ISBN 1-55755-166-9.
Suggested retail price $49.95 with companion CD-ROM.
Canadian $64.95.

To order direct call Toll Free 1-800-451-4319

In US and Canada add $5.00 shipping and handling. Foreign orders add $13.00 per item. Michigan residents add 4% sales tax.

Productivity Series books are for users who want to become more productive with their PC.

The Sound Blaster™ Book *Revised*

shows you how to use and explore the Sound Blaster™ card from Creative Labs. Sound Blaster™ is the popular interface that's used to produce music and sound effects.

The Sound Blaster™ Book is *the* guide to the Sound Blaster™ from installation to custom programming. You'll get an overview of the different Sound Blaster™ versions and the many different commercial, public domain and shareware software products that are available. One chapter is devoted to the MIDI standard and how to build a simple MIDI system.

The Sound Blaster Book is your ticket to the world of multimedia. After chapters dealing with the basics (installation, software, etc.), this book gets down to business: numerous programming examples enable you to transform your PC into a powerful sound machine.

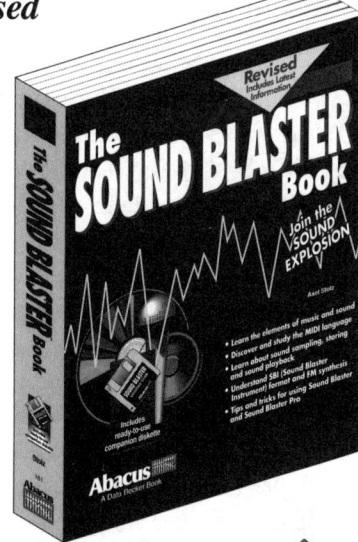

Other topics covered:
- Tips and tricks on Sound Blaster™1.0 through 2.0, Sound Blaster™ Pro and the new 16 ASP sound card.
- Software support for DOS and Windows
- MIDI with Sound Blaster™
- Programming the Sound Blaster card and much more!
- Also includes a companion diskette with valuable and useful programs for your Sound Blaster™

Author: Axel Stolz.
Order Item #B181. ISBN 1-55755-181-2.
Suggested retail price $34.95 with 3 ½" companion disk. Canadian $44.95.

To order direct call Toll Free 1-800-451-4319

In US and Canada add $5.00 shipping and handling. Foreign orders add $13.00 per item. Michigan residents add 4% sales tax.

Productivity Series books are for users who want to become more productive with their PC.

OS/2 2.1 Bible

IBM's new operating system, OS/2, sets new standards for PC operating systems. OS/2 promises a seamless interface for users of IBM's System Application Architecture. The **OS/2 Bible** explains the many features and tools that are part of this 32-bit multitasking system, its special functions, and the utilities that are part of the package. Whether you want to link simple DOS applications, run Windows programs under the Workplace Shell or understand the structure of OS/2 2.1 so you can optimally configure and optimize the System, **OS/2 Bible** covers all of these topics and more. The **OS/2 Bible** includes information on:

- Using the Enhanced Editor
- Using PM Chart
- Using the Icon Editor
- Using the OS/2 System Editor
- Using PM Diary
- The Multimedia Presentation Manager
- Using OS/2 in a Novell Network

Just a small sampling of the contents:

◆ Using the Boot Manager ◆ Partitioning the hard drive ◆ Installing device drivers ◆ Configuring your system ◆ Using the OS/2 utilities ◆ Introduction to OS/2 V2.1 basics ◆ Using Windows on the Desktop ◆ Windows and Menus ◆ The Games Folder ◆ The various configuration options ◆ Installing DOS programs ◆ Installing Windows applications ◆ Task control with REXX

Author(s): Robert Albrecht & Michael Plura
Order Item: #B174 ISBN: 1-55755-174-X
Suggested retail price: $34.95 US/ $44.95 CAN with companion diskette

To order direct call Toll Free 1-800-451-4319

In US and Canada add $5.00 shipping and handling. Foreign orders add $13.00 per item. Michigan residents add 4% sales tax.

Developers Series books are for professional software developers who require in-depth technical information and programming techniques.

Windows 3.1 Intern

This guide walks the you through the seemingly overwhelming tasks of writing Windows applications. It introduces you to the overall concept of Windows programming and events using dozens of easy to follow examples. It's a solid guide for intermediate to advanced Windows programmers. Topics include:

- The Windows message system
- Text and graphics output using Device Context
- Keyboard, mouse and timer input
- Memory management; Memory handles and RAM
- Printed output and Windows
- TrueType fonts
- Resources; menus, icons, dialog boxes and more
- Windows controls
- Standard dialog boxes
- Device-dependent and device-independent bitmaps
- File management under Windows

Order Item #B159. ISBN 1-55755-159-6.
Suggested retail price $49.95 with 3½" companion diskette.
Canadian $64.95.

To order direct call Toll Free 1-800-451-4319

In US and Canada add $5.00 shipping and handling. Foreign orders add $13.00 per item. Michigan residents add 4% sales tax.

Developers Series books are for professional software developers who require in-depth technical information and programming techniques.

PC Intern: System Programming
Second Edition
With updates for DOS 6.2 and Pentium

More than 400,000 programmers can't be wrong!

PC Intern has sold more than 400,000 copies to date. The new second edition **PC Intern** now includes important information on programming for the Pentium processor and for MS-DOS through version 6.2.

PC Intern is a literal encyclopedia for the DOS programmer. The book provides dozens of practical parallel working examples for programmers working in assembly language, C, Pascal, and BASIC. **PC Intern** clearly describes the technical aspects of programming under DOS. This book is part of our Developers Series which makes it a natural choice for professional software developers and those who want to be. The book's companion disk includes example programs shown in the book.

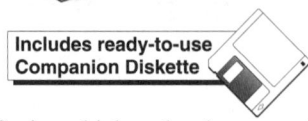

PC Intern: a thorough and comprehensive resource for PC programming.

Some of the topics covered are:

- Programming for the Pentium
- Programming unders MS-DOS 6.2
- Hardware and software interrupts
- COM and EXE programs
- BIOS fundamentals
- TSR programs
- Using extended and expanded memory
- PC memory organization
- Writing device drivers
- Multitasking
- DOS structures and functions
- Programming video cards

Includes ready-to-use Companion Diskette

Author: Michael Tischer
Order Item: #B145
ISBN: 1-55755-145-6
Suggested Retail Price: $59.95 US /$75.95 CAN with companion diskette

To order direct call Toll Free 1-800-451-4319

In US and Canada add $5.00 shipping and handling. Foreign orders add $13.00 per item. Michigan residents add 4% sales tax.

*Soft*Collection

Multimedia Dino Screen Saver for Windows --
featuring *Dino Motion*

They're back -- this time on your computer: Animated dinosaurs come back to life on your PC as lively screen savers. See the terrible T-Rex, Triceratops, Stegosaurus and more.

Multimedia Dino Screen Saver teaches you how to install and operate your new *Dino Motion* screen saver. It covers everything from installation to mastering the mixer -- how to speed up or slow down the action on the screen, how to attach dinosaur sounds to the appearance of each dinosaur, and how to insert or omit elements of the screen saver. You can customize the display of these prehistoric creatures with the *Dino Motion* mixer. It lets you go with or without sound effects, music and the animated background pictures and active volcanoes. The mixer gives you the option of picking one or two of your favorite dinosaurs or using all six of them at a time. *Dino Motion* lets you entertain yourself and prevent monitor damage at the same time!

Dino Motion features:
- ◆ Animated dinosaurs, plant life & volcanoes
- ◆ Mixer for custom settings
- ◆ Sound support for Windows WAV files

Multimedia Dino Screen Saver for Windows, featuring *Dino Motion*, is part of the *Soft*Collection, a new series of high quality, value-priced book/software combinations that fit everyone's budget. Each package in the series contains original software, NOT shareware. Our objective is to deliver targeted computing solutions in a book/software combination, featuring high-powered software without the high price.

Author: Thomas Stett
Order Item: #B240
ISBN: 1-55755-240-1
Suggested retail price: $12.95 US / $15.95 CAN with companion diskette

To order direct call Toll Free 1-800-451-4319

In US and Canada add $5.00 shipping and handling. Foreign orders add $13.00 per item. Michigan residents add 4% sales tax.

Amazing Software Tools that You Can Afford

SoftCollection

The Story Behind the *Soft*Collection

The *Soft*Collection is a new series of high quality, value-priced book/software combinations that fit everyone's budget. Each package in the series contains original software, not shareware. Our objective is to deliver targeted computing solutions in a book/software combination, featuring high powered software without the high price.

Available Now!:
Astrology on Your PC — *featuring Chinese Horoscope*
Personal Scheduler & Planner — *featuring Time & Date*
The Frugal Desktop Publisher — *featuring BeckerPage Lite*
Astronomy Star Finder for Windows — *featuring Sirius*
Raytrace Designer — *featuring Raytrace*
Manage DoubleSpace Compression from Windows — *featuring DoubleSpace Extensions*
E-Z Labels for Windows — *featuring Label Manager*
Multimedia Dino Screen Saver for Windows — *featuring Dino Motion*
Art Masterpieces — *featuring Art Collection*
Lighten Up with DTP Cartoon Characters — *featuring Cartoon Collection*
Add Impact with Business Graphics — *featuring Business Collection*
Computer Aided Design — *featuring CADPak Lite*
VIP Fax for Windows — *featuring VIP Fax*
Lightning Fast DOS — *featuring Tempest*

$12.95 — $19.95
($15.95 — $24.95 CAN)

Call Today for Your FREE *Soft*Collection Catalog!

To order direct call Toll Free 1-800-451-4319

In US and Canada add $5.00 shipping and handling. Foreign orders add $13.00 per item. Michigan residents add 4% sales tax.

Developers Series books are for professional software developers who require in-depth technical information and programming techniques.

PC Assembly Language Step by Step

For lightning execution speed, no computer language beats assembly language. This book teaches you PC assembly and machine language the right way - one step at a time. The companion diskette contains a unique simulator which shows you how each instruction functions as the PC executes it. Includes companion diskette containing assembly language simulator.

"I've yet to find a book which explains such a difficult language so well. This manual makes Assembly easy to learn." K.B., SC

"The book is a very practical introduction to PC assembly language programming. Anybody without computer know how can understand it." D.J., MI

"Very impressed with this book -Better than all the others I bought." C.S., CA

"This book is an exceptional training tool." J.L., TN

"Good, easy to understand book." S.S., NM

"An excellent introduction to assembly language." A.V., Austrailia

"Excellent, just the book I was looking for, easy to learn from." J.S., PA

"I learned a lot from this well written book." D.Z., OH

"Outstanding book! Incredibly clear, concise format. To the point!" J.C., HI

Order Item #B096. ISBN 1-55755-096-4.
Suggested retail price $34.95 with companion diskette.
Canadian $44.95.

To order direct call Toll Free 1-800-451-4319

In US and Canada add $5.00 shipping and handling. Foreign orders add $13.00 per item. Michigan residents add 4% sales tax.

DoubleSpace Without The DoubleTalk

Companion Diskette

The companion disk bundled with this book contains some great shareware data compression related utilities that will help ensure the integrity of your hard drive. At the time we went to press, the following three programs were lined up for the disk. See the README files first in case we've added more programs to the disk!

CheckIt PRO: CKMEDIA Applet

CKMEDIA can save you hours of downtime and megabytes of data loss due to undetected hard drive errors. With this program, you can avoid problems that might otherwise occur when installing and using DoubleSpace. **CKMEDIA** finds errors and physical media defects on hard drives, floppy drives or SyQuest/Bernoulli drives and produces a status report. You can then re-format or mark unsafe areas so they are not used by DoubleSpace.

To order the commercial version of this progam, contact:

TouchStone Software Corporation
2130 Main Street
Suite 250
Huntington Beach, CA 92648

Orders: (800) 531-0450 BBS: (714) 969-0688

Free Disk Space

All computer users want to know how much space is really available on their hard drives. **Free Disk Space** will scan all your connected drives (or just the ones you tell it to) and show you at a glance how much space is used and how much is still available. This includes all types of hard drives, RAM drives, network drives, CD ROM drives, Stacker drives, DoubleSpace drives and more. The Windows version (on our companion disk) features on-line help and allows you to view your used/free disk space in graphic or text mode.

Led's Stacker Directory (LSDIR)

A quick-fix answer to making a better Stacker directory command. **LSDIR** displays everything on the directory including Stacker drive/volume, not available through DOS commands. **LSDIR** also displays compression ratios in "PK-ZIP" fashion (e.g.: 76%) making it easier to understand.